CAF **HOW TO** GUIDE

RUNNING

A

LOCAL

FUNDRAISING

CAMPAIGN

A guide for absolute beginners

JANET HILDERLEY

GW00725450

CAF

Published by Charities Aid Foundation
Kings Hill
West Malling
Kent ME19 4TA

Editors   Nina Behrman and Kate Swainson

Design and production   Eugenie Dodd Typographics

Printed and bound in Great Britain by Bell & Bain Limited, Glasgow

A catalogue record for this book is available from the British Library.

ISBN 1–85934–040–7

Telephone   +44 (0) 1732 520000
Fax   +44 (0) 1732 520001
E-mail   Cafpubs@CAF.charitynet.org

CAF's web page:
http://www.charitynet.org

*No responsibility for loss occasioned to any person acting or refraining from
action as a result of the material in this publication can be accepted by the
Charities Aid Foundation.*

*The author and publishers are grateful to Jennie Whiting for her
useful comments and suggestions.*

Contents

About the author
·········

Janet Hilderley worked in promotion management in the
oil, hotel and publishing industries before forming her own
company in 1989, Janet Hilderley Associates. Her last positions
have been as head of fundraising for two leading charities.
Working with local charities during the recession, Janet found
that a different approach was needed with the many charities
which had lost long-time supporters and were in financial
difficulties.

Janet was impressed by the dedication of the staff and the way
that client needs focused workers' attention. Clients included
the Disabled Living Foundation, St James' Church, Piccadilly,
the Trevor Jones Trust, branches of the Motor Neurone
Disease Association and The Samaritans. Janet is currently
concentrating on writing on charity matters.

Preface

Local fundraising is fun but if like me you come to it from a professional or business environment, or even a high-powered national charity, then you are in for a culture shock. My first experience of local fundraising was working with a man who had raised over £30 million for an international charity. We organised a house-to-house collection for a small regional charity. We found ourselves stuffing the envelopes – because our 'staff' had gone to the dentist. You will not have the back-up financially or administratively and you cannot spend money to make money. But to raise funds for a cause with which you can identify is one hundred per cent satisfying.

Local fundraising is networking, dealing with local people, knowing your patch and making sure that people know about your work; you must cultivate contacts with the media. It is also knowing that not everybody is as decent and honest as you are. There may be a Trustee who travels via John O'Groats when claiming expenses or an honest person who knows nothing of fundraising ethics and takes money off for their time.

This book is intended to meet the requirements of somebody coming to local fundraising for the first time, whether they are a professional fundraiser, taking over a charity, a doctor needing funds for the 'blood run', or a member of the village cricket team. This is a book of ideas and support: whatever your fundraising need, this book is for you. GOOD LUCK all the way.

Janet Hilderley
May 1997

Introduction
·········

In this book, local fundraising means raising funds from local sources, for a local charity or campaign, or for a local branch of a national charity. As a local fundraiser, you may not have the benefit of a nationally or even internationally known name behind you, nor will you have the benefit of expert help and advice, office space, high-tech equipment and – most of all – access to funds. You will have to make much more use of your own initiative.

Whether you are fundraising as a volunteer or a paid staff member, you could be very much on your own, but this book will be your companion and adviser. The book is written for complete beginners in local fundraising, and no prior knowledge is assumed. It is not about quick fixes (although sometimes they can happen). The aim of this book is to guide you if you are new to fundraising, or perhaps new to the charity world, but have been dropped in at the deep end. The book is appropriate for new charities starting up, existing local charities working without much support, or local branches of a national charity where fundraisers may feel rather remote from the centre.

Essentially a practical guide, this book begins by taking you through the fundamentals – basic requirements of office space, equipment and staff, how to find start-up funding, what you need to find out, and how to create an effective fundraising plan.

Twelve different fundraising techniques or sources of funds are then explained. Don't worry – you don't need to use all of them, but this is a range for you to select from. What you use depends on you, your resources, your local situation, and why you need the money – for running expenses, to build up your capital or for a special project.

The last two chapters guide you through ways to publicise your charity or project, monitor your results, and plan for the future. A bibliography and detailed appendices offer sources of further information and training, sample letters, and summaries of essential, relevant aspects of charity law and taxation.

CHAPTER ONE

Assessing your resources

Before you start working on your campaign or fundraising activities, it is important to take stock of your resources – of all kinds – and consider some preliminary basic steps such as start-up funding, becoming a registered charity or forming a fundraising committee.

Your resources

Your own skills

As a local fundraiser, you will need lots of common sense, enthusiasm, adaptability and staying power. It will help if you also have a mix of business skills and experience (possibly, but by no means essentially, including marketing and public relations). It is also important to identify any gaps in expertise or experience where training may be required.

Fundraising for a good cause is an immensely fulfilling and satisfying occupation. Unfortunately however, not everyone in fundraising is as decent and honest as you are and you will need to be streetwise enough to spot would-be helpers who are using the cover of your charity for their own ends. Many charities, and the charity sector in general, have received bad publicity from people taking advantage in this way. (Detailed guidance on ethics and good practice is available from the Institute of Charity Fundraising Managers, ICFM, as listed in Appendix I.)

Start-up funds

This can be a chicken-and-egg situation: you need charitable status before you can apply for start-up funds and yet you may need some funding before you have achieved charitable status. Provided that you can establish your genuine intentions, you can print 'charitable status applied for' on your stationery and literature, and make application to some of the organisations listed below. (Addresses and telephone numbers are included in Appendix I.)

- The Charities Aid Foundation (CAF) is the leading non-government organisation working for charity, and is itself a charity. CAF may give you a six-month grant for payment towards a fundraiser's salary.

- CAF also now operates a loan scheme, Investors in Society, whereby individuals and businesses will lend money to charities at no interest.

- Charity Projects – probably best known for organising 'Red Nose Day' – may also help with start-up funds.

- Grant-making trusts (see Chapter 14) may help with start-up operations.

- Local companies may also be prepared to help. They may want their name linked with your charity, or might be quite content to remain in the background. *Who Owns Whom* (see Bibliography) will alert you if an apparently local business belongs to a conglomerate with an interest which may conflict with your charity's aims.

You may need to wait six months to a year for your start-up funds to materialise unless a local company, or even a generous individual, is prepared to move quickly.

Registration status

To become a registered charity, you must apply to the Charity Commission, responsible to the government for administering and monitoring the charity industry (address in Appendix I).

Publicity material

If you're starting a new charity or campaign, Chapter 16 offers information on creating publicity material. If you have moved into an existing charity, you must be ruthless: take a long hard look at the publicity material you have inherited. If it does not state clearly who you are, what you do, and why, it can only be a false economy to use it 'just for the time being'.

Basic needs

Physical

Have you got any premises? What are you going to use for an office? How are you going to get hold of furniture and office equipment when you have no money? You may need to find a sponsor to help with the equipment or even premises: a kind bank manager or an understanding shop manager or proprietor might support you (see Chapter 9, Local business support).

Personnel

You cannot do everything on your own. You will have to build a team, taking the greatest possible care to ensure that other people are joining you for the right reasons. At first your team members will have to be volunteers (people who are prepared to donate their time for helping a charity). Good volunteers are like gold dust and should be valued and thanked regularly.

Volunteers can be found through the following:

- REACH (Retired Executives Action Clearing House) holds lists of retired senior professionals and business people willing to do volunteer work; they have regional offices all over the UK.

- The Voluntary Service Bureau (VSB) has a register of volunteers of all ages. Look in the *Yellow Pages* for your local address.

- Other possible sources include churches and other religious institutions; local organisations such as Soroptimists, Rotary, Women's Institutes and the Townswomen's Guild;

and making appeals for volunteers through local radio stations and newspapers.

Addresses of organisations mentioned above are listed in Appendix I.

The fundraising committee

You are now juggling many roles at once. While you are doing your research (see Chapter 2) you will be meeting potentially supportive and influential local people who could form the nucleus of your fundraising committee. You should be courting them.

Chairperson

Whether you find your chairperson first, or get together a committee and let them elect one, is a matter of style and circumstances. If you are a committee member, you may be able to exert influence on the selection of the chairperson. The chairperson must: be able to chair a meeting and control the other committee members; have a charismatic personality; be a good listener and a persuasive speaker; and have sufficient time to devote to the cause.

Secretary and/or administrator

The roles of committee secretary and administrator will probably be filled by you if you are starting a charity, until you can afford to pay someone else or find a suitably qualified volunteer. The secretary organises committee meetings and keeps the minutes.

Treasurer

To avoid any conflict of interest, neither the chairperson nor the finance director of the charity should take on this task. It is necessary that the overall income of the charity is not agreed and signed as being accurate by the same person or people who have been raising it. Otherwise, there is too much opportunity for errors or abuse. Ideally the treasurer should be someone with financial experience such as an accountant or a bank manager who can control the funds and give the project integrity. He or she should be able to take over from the chairperson if necessary and should be sufficiently vigorous to control the committee members' expenses which can get out of hand!

Committee members

As a group, the committee members should possess a mix of skills and interests. For example, this could be found in a committee consisting of a retailer, a publican, a marketing or public relations person, and a few other well-connected local people.

Important points to remember:

- In practice, some, if not most, of the members of your fundraising committee may also be Trustees as members of the charity's main management committee.

- Any of your key committee members may resign or move on at any time. Always have a suitable successor in mind. (This is called succession management.)

- Try to ensure that *all* your committee members are loyal to your cause.

A patron

Once your fundraising committee is established, and you are up and running, it can help enormously to have a patron. Some of the big national charities have a member of the Royal Family as their patron. A local charity has to set its sights rather lower but you might ask a captain of industry who lives locally, a distinguished local aristocrat, a politician or a well-known sports or show-business personality who is prepared to lend his or her name to your charity.

The duties are not onerous: the patron's name is printed on the charity's letterhead, and he or she can provide support by attending special events organised by the charity. (Sometimes it happens that a patron can become far more involved than this. For example, Lord Rix was patron of MENCAP but was so interested that he became its very active chairman and found a second career!)

KEY POINTS
• • • • • • • • •

- Can you find sufficient funds to keep going? Consult your treasurer and find a sponsor.

- Are you a registered charity or have you applied for registration?

- Have you premises, equipment and staff (either volunteers or paid)?

- Are you confident that any existing pledges of time or money will be fulfilled?

- Do you have the unstinting support of your committee members?

• • • • • • • • •

CHAPTER TWO

Research

Before you decide on fundraising methods, and start working with them, it is essential to make sure that you choose the right methods and the right targets. Some background research is essential for learning more about your local people, and how they regard your charity.

What kind of research?

There are two types of research which may be relevant: desk research (also euphemistically known as 'legwork'); and the sort carried out by market research companies using paid interviewers. Desk research means finding out as much as you can by looking in reference books and keeping an eye on the local papers, all of which you can do yourself.

Some charities may be able to persuade a market research company to carry out a small investigation on their behalf – possibly riding on the back of a larger research study. In most local fundraising contexts, professional market research is prohibitively expensive.

Market research companies tend to be located in the major conurbations; you can order a list of companies from the Market Research Society (address in Appendix I) for a small fee. You may be able to obtain information on local companies more easily if you have someone in the marketing business on your fundraising committee.

Your charity's reputation

You must establish that your charity's name is known locally; if, however, your project is better known than the charity, this need not be a bad thing. Your project has more chance of success if it is known, as well as if it is understood and supported by local people. If necessary, you can change the emphasis of the project to adapt to local concerns, as revealed by your research.

CASE NOTE

Your charity is newly resurrected from the Young Persons' Metropolitan Recreation and Relief Society. This name reflects the charity's Victorian origins. Because the aim of the new form of the charity is to raise money for a swimming pool and fitness centre, you may be more successful in fundraising against a more modern-sounding name such as 'The King Street Swimming Pool and Fitness Centre Project', and/or perhaps a shorter name such as 'Splash'.

Finding out whether your charity or project is sufficiently well known can be quite a simple task which could be accomplished by you and perhaps one or two of your committee members speaking informally to as many people as possible in your area over the course of a week or two. If you wanted to be more sophisticated, you could use a simple questionnaire, such as the example shown opposite.

Some sort of enquiry is essential if you are seeking to ascertain whether a new charity is establishing a reputation. It is also useful to have a 'baseline' measure before a publicity campaign, against which to assess the results of publicity techniques.

The research questionnaire is not absolutely essential but should give you more reliable results which you could analyse for your future publicity planning.

Suggested research questionnaire

NOTES TO INTERVIEWER: try to interview 50 people (25 men and 25 women). Do not ask their ages but using your own judgement try to find about 5 in each of these age groups: 16–24, 25–34, 35–44, 45–64, and 65 or over.

I am carrying out a small enquiry on behalf of a local charity as we want to find out if we are becoming known in the area. Please may I ask you a few questions?

1 *[Show letter heading]* This is our letter heading. Had you ever heard of [Charity name] before I showed this to you? yes/no *(delete according to answer)*

2 What do you think we do? _____

3 How long do you think we have been established? Less than a year □ Between one and two years □ Over two years □ *(tick appropriate box)*

   (the timescale can be adjusted according to the age of your charity)

4 We are raising money for [project name/aim]. I am not asking you for money now, but is this the sort of cause you would want to support? yes/no

5 Could you say why? _____

6 *(If answer to question 1 or 4 was 'Yes' ask:)* Where have you heard of us? Radio □ Poster □ Leaflet □ Local paper □ Seen our shop □ Word of mouth □ Other _____

   (interviewer – tick more than one if necessary)

To be completed by interviewer: Male/female Approximate age group _____

This is not a particularly 'easy' questionnaire because some of the questions are open-ended, so you need to recruit intelligent interviewers (perhaps only one person other than yourself) and make sure that they are briefed very carefully.

Question 4 is very important because you also want to be sure that the actual 'need' has sufficient appeal locally. Let us suppose that you are raising money to improve an open space but no one is turned on by this. You could change the description of the appeal to 'Planting trees for tomorrow – your children's heritage', for example.

Desk research

Background

Key sources and techniques for 'desk research' include the following:

- The reference section of your local library. Books such as *Who Owns Whom* can show you that a 'local' retailer is part of a national chain (though retaining a separate name). Other useful titles include: *Debrett's People of Today*, *A Guide to Local Charitable Trusts*, *Charities Digest* (a list of large and medium-sized UK charities and what they do), and *Hollis Sponsorship and Donations Yearbook* (which lists who has sponsored which charity). (See Bibliography for details.)

- The business information section of a larger public library. Computerised access to company information (such as chairperson, turnover, number of staff) may be available free of charge.

- The telephone. A phone call is quicker and cheaper than writing a letter. A fax can cost even less.

- Your own charity's records, if the charity is already established. You should know who your current supporters are and what they have donated in the past. And they should know that an enthusiastic new broom – you – has arrived!

- Other charities: a national charity such as Help the Aged, for example, may even help you with start-up funds if you are establishing a new charity for older people. Perhaps you could help another local charity in turn with your expertise?

Competing interests

It is generally wise to be aware of the other local fundraising or promotional activities in your area, if only to avoid clashing with them. However, interests which appear competing can also be complementary.

- Store promotions: find out what the big stores are up to in order to avoid the high spot of your appeal competing with a major store promotion, especially a sale. On the other hand, you might be able to tie in with their promotion (see Chapter 16, Publicity techniques).

- Blockbuster movies: do not let a big film promotion clash with your event. If possible, find out about any promotions in advance. It may be appropriate to arrange some spin-off if you can – a charity film evening, for example.

- You don't need to research Christmas shopping, but be aware of it in your planning. Although it is a time of high expenditure for most people, many are more generous at Christmas time. It is indeed the season of goodwill!

Your locality

The local economy

Is your area expanding economically, or going through hard times? The problem is that the harder things are, the more you need the money, and the more difficult it is to get.

You can find out what is happening and what is *going* to happen locally by talking to your bank manager, newspaper editors and the finance director of the local authority. Between them they should know about forthcoming government plans, which major companies are moving in or out of the neighbourhood, new road and housing developments – possibly even new towns.

Local demography

You need to know the class, age and sex breakdown of the local population, especially if it is very different from the population as a whole. Crucially, and related to this, you need to identify where the money is (as we shall see in Chapters 5 and 6 on direct mail and telephone appeals). In general, older people have more uncommitted money than young people; older women are major legacy givers; and young women enjoy events.

You can find demographic information in your local government office. The staff in your local public library may also be able to help. The advertising manager of your local paper can often be helpful as a user of this type of information in the sale of advertising space.

Support from local businesses and local government

This is where you are going to be doing a lot of legwork and telephoning. These sources are sufficiently important to merit whole chapters later in this book (see Chapters 9, 13 and 15).

Religious organisations

There may be many different places of worship in your area, and sometimes many different religions. Make it your business to visit all the incumbents: make sure that they know about your cause and find out about their attitudes and what *their* needs are. If yours is a specifically religious charity, the same rule applies.

Support from religious organisations gives your cause respect, and participants at religious centres are part of the local networking system. They may also be good sources of legacies (see Chapter 12, Legacies).

Marketing day

A marketing day is a useful way of getting to know who's who in your community and letting them know who you are.

As mentioned in Chapter 1, establishing a fundraising committee is an important early step for a new charity or campaign. The committee members, plus others who know the area and can spare a day but are not prepared to join the committee, can form the nucleus of a brainstorming group who really know the area. The ideal group size is 12–15 people.

The session should be very informal, but you could set yourself a loose agenda covering:

- aims and objectives (it is important to agree these early on, and make sure that they are understood by all concerned);

- possible patron or local celebrity supporters, and where they live;
- potential sources of funds;
- who is who in the business community;
- attitudes of the media;
- potentially popular new events;
- existing events which your charity could sponsor;
- local landmarks (useful for arranging street collections, for example);
- the history of successful and unsuccessful appeals;
- places of worship, schools and other community centres.

Formal minutes are not usually required, but someone (probably you) should keep a record of the salient points, or perhaps record the proceedings on tape. This is a matter of your own style.

One way to start a marketing day is to ask everyone to introduce themselves and say what experience any of them might have of raising money in any field. A large map of the area (which may be a gift in kind from a local shop) can be useful. It may be helpful to write key points on a board or flipchart as you go along.

At the end of the day, careful analysis of all the information gathered can be very helpful.

CASE NOTE
. . . .
A local charity for people with learning disabilities had a marketing day. They learnt from the Chamber of Commerce which were the more successful local businesses, and researched where the 'in' pubs were, as planned. But what also emerged was that a grandmother of one of the brainstormers lived next door to a grandmother of an Olympic ice-skating champion. This led to the skater being guest of honour at what was to become a high-profile event. The same brainstorming group also found out that an internationally famous film star had a nephew with a learning disability living in the area, and the film star lent his name to the cause.
. . . .

Background information

. . . .

There are other sources you can tap into to collect further information.

Local

. . . .

- Voluntary Service Bureau (VSB): the local charity support and advice centre.

- Chamber of Commerce: an association of local business people and professionals who group together to improve the business climate in the community. The Chambers are usually central to local business life.

- Business colleges: these are usually in touch with local business and can provide skills such as helping produce a promotional video.

Charity industry

. . . .

- The National Council for Voluntary Organisations (NCVO) has an excellent library and lists of consultants who can help you if you can afford to employ them.

- The Institute of Charity Fundraising Managers (ICFM) can provide advice on raising money.

- The Charities Aid Foundation (CAF) sells useful publications and can provide advice on ways of giving. CAF also holds courses on training and keeping volunteers and on particular aspects of fundraising.

- The National Association of Councils of Voluntary Service (NACVS) will give you the addresses of local Voluntary Service Councils (VSCs) giving further back-up to local charities.

- The Royal Association for Disability and Rehabilitation (RADAR) is the umbrella charity for people with disabilities. Individual charities can join as group members.

- The British Association of Settlements and Social Action Centres (BASSAC) has a lot of expertise in local community work. Again, individuals or charities can join.

- Help the Aged and Age Concern can offer advice and support to local charities.

You will find the addresses and telephone numbers of these organisations in Appendix I.

General

- The Sports Council is the co-ordinating organisation for all sporting activities and facilities.

- The Home Office is the ministry responsible for charities, but the voluntary services unit of the Home Office now reports to the Department of Heritage.

KEY POINTS

- How well known is your charity or cause?

- How can you find out?

- Where you will find background information?

- What you have found out?

- Benefits of holding a marketing day.

CHAPTER THREE

The fundraising plan

Having assessed your resources and researched your area in depth, you next need to work out your strategy for raising the money – and should therefore create a written fundraising plan. The proficiency of your charity may well be judged by the professionalism of the plan.

When the plan is completed you should send copies to your bank manager, your patron and the fundraising committee members (who in practice will have helped with its preparation). Be prepared also to give copies to would-be major supporters who may wish to see evidence of your professionalism.

What should the plan include?

The fundraising plan should include the following basic elements of information about your charity, the funds requested, and your fundraising strategy.

The charity or project

- Background – why the charity was formed, by whom and when.
- The aims and objectives of the charity or project.
- Who the beneficiaries will be and how many there could be.
- Geographic area covered.
- If already established, achievements to date.

The funds to be raised

- Why is the money needed. This could be for a capital appeal, a specific project, or running costs, including 'expenses'.

- How much is needed.

- The timescale and any schedule of funds required.

- How the money will be spent. This should be broken down in great detail (and include projections for 'expenses': where estimates have been received these should be itemised and quoted. If you need a stair-lift, say why; if you need a multigym, say why. Do not generalise – funders will see through the flannel. Always explain why you want what you have requested.

CASE NOTE

Funders can guide charities towards sympathetic suppliers. For example, when wood was specified for a building project the funder was able to recommend a supplier who gives favourable terms to charities.

Other considerations

- Popularity of your appeal – is it an emotive call for help that will immediately appeal to potential donors?

- If your need is vital, but not necessarily charismatic, can you make it more appealing?

- Competing interests – consider any other projects or activities which may be competing for the same funds. What is special about your appeal? Does it fill a gap? Is it unique? If you can't answer 'yes' to any of these perhaps you should not be running an appeal, or even your charity! Make sure the fundraising plan includes an explanation of what is unique about your project.

CASE NOTE

A country church needed £250,000 for re-roofing and other major repairs and increased accommodation. Research showed that local funders were unmoved. When it was projected as a counselling centre, a local resource centre which housed archive material, and a crèche, the funders responded.

· · · · · · · · ·

Targeting

Whom should you target as potential funders? (For example, an appeal for sports facilities may not attract the same people as an appeal for an organ fund.) Consider:

- wealthy individuals;
- young achievers;
- companies;
- charitable trusts;
- local associations.

You will find targeting easier if you have obtained demographic breakdowns of your area in terms of age, sex and social class either from the council or from your local library (see Chapter 2). This can be included in the fundraising plan.

Media selection

As you go through this book you will find out more about the many media where you can place your message: sometimes you will have to pay, but you may often be able to arrange for free publicity (see Chapter 16, Publicity techniques). Your plan should show which media you intend to use, and projected expenditure on those selected from:

- press and radio advertising;
- posters;
- telephoning;
- door-to-door collecting;
- events;
- leaflets;
- direct mail.

The summary table at the end of this chapter offers a guide to choosing media and methods.

'Hidden' resources

You may also have 'hidden' resources which you have carefully cultivated, even if they do not form part of your written fundraising plan: use these to get all the free publicity you possibly can. They may include:

- local newspaper and radio contacts;
- local business and community contacts;
- your own and your committee's expertise and contacts.

Projections

Your plan should end with your monthly financial projections, which you should work out with the help of your treasurer, broken down into:

- known income from covenants and other regular or predictable payments;
- projected income;
- the 'target' to achieve your budget (NB 'target' is always higher than 'budget');
- 'budget' – the amount you actually require;
- 'cash flow' – in practice the money will not come in at an even rate so the 'cash flow' projections will show how you are really doing against your target.

Summary of fundraising options

This is a summary of the fundraising methods and sources of funding covered in this book.

Chapter number	Option	Timescale	Whom to approach	Who does the work
4	Events	6–12 months	Companies, press, celebrities, patron	Skilled organisers, volunteers
5	Direct mail	Immediate	Individuals	Volunteers to stuff envelopes, a 'signature'
6	Telephone	Immediate	Individuals	Students, people with past experience, volunteers
7	Collections (house-to-house & street)	1–3 months	Pub & shop managers, relevant local authorities	Students, volunteers, local people
8	Radio or newspaper	Immediate	Editor, promotions editor	Patron, celebrities, good voices
9	Local	1–2 years	Marketing directors	Volunteers, professionals, business support (bank managers are ideal), MDs & chairs of smaller companies
9	Associations & organisations, schools	Can be immediate	Association secretaries, headteachers	People with presence and good presentation skills

10	Shops	Can be immediate; allow 1 month for setting-up time	Associations, advertising departments of local press	Volunteers, manager with retail experience
11	Donations	Immediate or long term	Individuals, companies, trusts	Professional people, volunteers
12	Legacies	Long term	Older people	Volunteers & professionals
13	Local authorities	6–12 months	Grant-giving committee	Professional people, volunteers
14	Charitable	6–12 months	Correspondent (secretary)	Solicitors, volunteers, trusts (bank managers are ideal)

CHAPTER FOUR

Events

Events may be the public face of a charity, but they are not usually its biggest source of income. They are also very time-consuming and possibly risky. The advantages of holding an event are that it can help to put your charity on the map, and all involved get a huge glow of satisfaction from a successful event. This can result in extra energy going into the more mundane, but potentially more profitable, forms of fundraising which can pay dividends for months to come.

Initial considerations

The type of event chosen should be appropriate for the target audience and fit in well with other events and local interests. You therefore need to conduct rigorous research.

Who does the organising?

The big charities often employ a full-time event organiser – sometimes even more than one – or hire consultants. At a local scale, you will probably find that you are the event organiser for your charity, unless you can find a volunteer with sufficient experience and enthusiasm. You might decide to hire a consultant for an agreed fee, but you would need to be very sure that this would be cost-effective. The Institute of Charity Fundraising Management (ICFM) publishes *Guidelines on Employing a Consultant*.

Event committee

If you are planning an ambitious event you should set up an event committee which could attract people with the right sort of organising, sales and publicity skills. If you plan to have an event programme which can increase your revenue through sales of advertising space you will also need someone on your committee who can co-ordinate production and organise selling the advertising space (see Chapter 16, Publicity techniques).

As with the fundraising committee (see Chapter 1), the event committee should elect its own chairperson (unless you have already appointed one); you should remain on the committee as secretary.

Objectives

While the obvious objective of an event is to raise money, there is often also a hidden agenda of other benefits:

- to attract the media and establish the reputation of your fledgling charity;
- to persuade any would-be patron that you are a charity worth supporting;
- volunteers enjoy events: many will get involved for the first time at an event, and some may remain with you for the more mundane, everyday work of fundraising;
- sponsors and donors, whom you will almost certainly need to cover the setting-up costs, may be more likely to come forward to help you.

Resources

Do you have sufficient funds to hold the event? You must not commit yourself to any expenditure unless you are covered. Tempting as it is to get the show on the road, your first task is to cover your costs, as indicated in the operating plan below. A sponsor may be able to underwrite the event.

Do you have the skills and the person hours available – your own and/or those of an experienced volunteer or consultant?

An abandoned event is one of the worst things that can happen to your charity – or to you!

Types of event

There are many types of event, from a whist drive to a gala dinner and ball. Some are more suited to a national charity, and all have advantages and disadvantages. There are too many to list here but the Bibliography at the back of this book includes some sources of further information.

CASE NOTE

St James' Church, Piccadilly, has a unique Grinling Gibbons altarpiece, which was collapsing. The church was lit by candlelight for an up-market dinner. The unusual setting attracted wealthy donors who could see the need for restoration of the carving.

Shared events

Sometimes it may make sense to share an event with another local charity. A local group or association such as the Lions may be running an event and actively seeking a charity to come in with them (see Chapter 9, Local business support).

CASE NOTE

The Young Lions helped a small charity to organise a major horse show: they sold tickets, found sponsors and helped with the administration. The result was a splendid and highly successful event which provided much-wanted funds for a needy charity.

Outline operating plan

One year ahead (yes, this is the timescale you should allow!):

- decide on the type of event you are planning;
- draft an approximate timetable;
- prepare a rough budget with break-even and cut-off points (it is important not to go beyond a cut-off point if there is not enough interest or money coming in);

- talk to potential sponsors (the Chamber of Commerce may be able to guide you);
- reserve, but do not confirm, your venue (or alternatives);
- contact suppliers such as caterers, florists, marquee hirers, companies that hire public address systems, etc, and make provisional bookings.

Six months in advance:

- confirm bookings for caterers, etc;
- a sales team for programme advertising should be in place;
- if the scale of the event justifies the investment, order special 'event' stationery;
- recruit and book volunteers.

Three months in advance:

- finalise the timetable;
- apply for a special licence if you need one (see Appendix II);
- order transport;
- complete arrangements for raffles, tombolas or auctions.

One month before the event:

- double-check everything weekly and more often as you get closer;
- give every team-member written instructions, and have them signed as understood.

One week before:

- check that all your suppliers are ready to go;
- re-read the brief so you know it intimately.

On the day:

- like an actor, you must know your part inside out;
- do not allocate specific tasks to yourself, but concentrate on ensuring that everyone else does their job and that things run smoothly;
- carry your time-sheet with you (a clipboard is ideal for holding it);

- make sure all your volunteers are present and know their responsibilities;
- make sure your celebrity has arrived and does not 'disappear';
- keep control and never show panic.

CASE NOTE

One organiser of an event in a theatre had all the scenery collapse on her and had to run all round the site in order to arrive with the prizes. The audience thought it was pre-planned!

Risk

Insurance

All events have an element of risk: a celebrity may not turn up, rain may stop people coming, roads may be closed. Insurance is a must! Cornhill Insurance (address in Appendix I) is one company which can provide cover for most types of event. You must also have public liability insurance, and you would be wise to discuss this with a broker.

Food and drink

If you are providing food it is best to talk first to the health department of your local authority as the regulations they publish can be difficult to interpret (and see Appendix II). If you are serving alcoholic drinks and the venue is unlicensed you will need to go to your local magistrates' court for a licence. The court is almost always prepared to give you helpful advice before you apply.

ADVANTAGES

- Events almost invariably have a high profile.
- They attract new sponsors, supporters and volunteers, and are popular.
- Patrons and important supporters enjoy events.
- A successful event boosts staff morale, which may have long-term benefits.

DISADVANTAGES
....
- By nature, events are labour-intensive.
- You can never completely eliminate the element of risk.
- You will need to find money in advance.

RESOURCES
....
- A sponsor can underwrite the event.
- Many hard-working volunteers are essential.
- The event must be co-ordinated by an experienced organiser.
- Patron or celebrity endorsement will attract other people.

PUBLICITY
....
- You should try and get your posters displayed everywhere you can without paying: libraries, supermarkets, public houses and of course in your own charity shop.
- Enclose your event leaflets with every letter you send out, and place them on counters, in reception areas and everywhere they are accepted, and, if you can arrange it, deliver them door-to-door.
- Negotiate free mentions on local radio and in the local press.

(See also Chapter 16, Publicity techniques.)

KEY POINTS
....
- Establish an event committee.
- Clarify your objectives.
- Have you sufficient start-up funds or do you need sponsorship?
- Have you sufficient non-financial resources?
- Events don't just happen: have you a skilled and experienced organiser plus sufficient volunteers?
- Has the proposed event got sufficient 'appeal'?
- Are you fully insured? Have you minimised the unavoidable element of risk?
....

CHAPTER FIVE

Direct mail

Direct mail is the term used for writing to large numbers of people at the same time, and, in the case of charities, asking them for money. Many of the large charities use direct mail almost continuously. If you are on their mailing lists, you probably receive charity appeal letters – some of which are very ingenious – several times a month. They are not sent at random: addresses are carefully selected from those who have supported charities in the past; people who live in up-market areas, and people who are known to have attended charity events.

The financial services industry also uses direct mail to sell unit trust issues, offer loans, sell hospital insurance plans, and much else besides. All this, particularly in urban areas, has to compete with hand deliveries put through your door by local mini-cab companies, pizza delivery firms, roof repairers, and many others. Many people lump all unsolicited mail together as 'junk mail'.

To stand out in this crowded marketplace both your targeting and the quality of your mailing has to be outstanding. However, you have two very great advantages: your appeal is local, and it is for a good cause, so you will establish an immediate rapport with your audience – particularly if you have made sure that your charity is well known in your area.

The ingredients of success

Targeting

Unless yours is a very special case with universal appeal, your mailing should be targeted at the more prosperous homes in your area, but if, for example, you're making an appeal on behalf of a sporting charity then you should be targeting members of sports clubs as well.

You will know from your research (see Chapter 2) where the more prosperous people in your area live. You can find their addresses from the electoral rolls at the council offices or in your local library. Some of the more enlightened councils should be able to sell you pre-printed sticky labels (a guide price for labels from a London borough is £85 per thousand). Some councils will supply the lists on computer disk (guide price about £25 per thousand) from which you can print your own labels.

Provided that you have built up a good relationship with them, secretaries of sports clubs or other special interest groups may supply you with address labels or lists. Neither councils nor clubs are always willing to give out the actual disks – though you can sometimes make copies of the electoral roll in your library.

If you are getting names from more than one source it is important to avoid mailing the same person more than once, which can aggravate them. If you have the time and the opportunity you can use your computer to alphabetise the list and you will then be able to spot any duplication.

CASE NOTE

Back in the 1950s a cigarette company was launching an expensive new brand of cigarettes and decided to mail a sample pack to the great and the good – known as 'opinion formers'. The Queen's then racehorse trainer received no fewer than four mailings. He was not grateful for the free cigarettes – he was furious!

Also avoid mailing dead people. Understandably, this does not go down well either! You can have someone check the obituaries and death announcements, and amend your records accordingly, but this is very time-consuming and minimally effective – hardly worth the candle! If you do find out that you have mailed a dead person take him or her off your list immediately. One charity continued mailing a dead person for twenty years!

The message

You should consider using direct mail only if you have something of real interest to write about before you attempt to ask people to get out their cheque books. You can of course invent the interest (eg 'Did you know that the world's fastest animal, the cheetah, can cover the ground at 60mph?') but your taster must whet the appetite and you must make it relevant.

You must also be absolutely sure why you want the money, and say so in the letter.

The letter

The letter is a vitally important ingredient. This book cannot make you into a good letter-writer but we can point out the main ingredients, and to help we quote as an inspiration several letters known to have been successful (see Appendix III).

Personalised letters work best but this means extra time and expense, especially if you are sending out letters by the hundred. You may wish to do a test before undertaking this time-consuming extra task. For example, try sending out 500 personalised letters, and 500 non-personalised, to as uniform a target group as possible. Is there a significant difference in response? One good way of starting letters (which saves personalising) used by many charities is 'Dear Friend'.

You can sub-contract the whole direct mail operation to a direct mail contractor (see Appendix I) which will provide you with mailing lists, suggest ideas, write the letter, personalise the mailings (if you do decide to go to the extra expense), address the envelopes and 'stuff' them (put in the enclosures) for you. However, this is expensive and unlikely to be cost-effective unless you are doing a national mailing. Volunteers can take on these tasks, including personalising the letters, if you decide to do this.

It can save money if you print your letter headings at the same time as your letter. If there is black in the letterhead design print the text of the letter at the same time, and if the letterhead design uses blue (or another suitable colour) print the signature at the same time.

Depending on your target audience, longer letters with more than one page can be more effective, and several enclosures – often repeating a similar message with a different slant – can help to get a higher response, but again these all cost money which you may not yet have. People of lower social classes tend to enjoy 'thumbing through' enclosures, research shows, while 'ABC1s' may prefer more concise mailings.

Donation form

What is cost-effective – and strongly recommended – is to enclose a donation form providing for cheque, postal order, money order and, most important of all, credit card donations. An example is shown overleaf. The form can also include examples of what could be provided with different amounts donated, for example '£12 will provide vitamins for a child for one year'.

Donation form

I would like to give the sum of:

£12 ☐ £20 ☐ £50 ☐ £100 ☐ £250 ☐ I prefer to give £ _____

I enclose my Cheque ☐ Postal Order ☐ Money Order ☐
CAF Voucher ☐ *(Cheques/Postal Order/Money Order/CAF Voucher made payable to 'your charity name')*

or debit my Visa ☐ Mastercard ☐ Switch ☐ Other_____ ☐
(Please fill in)

Card No: ☐☐☐☐☐☐☐☐☐☐☐☐☐☐☐☐

Expiry Date: _____ Signature: _____

Please send this form together with your gift, in the reply-paid envelope provided, to: **Your Charity Name**, **Freepost**, Your address in full including **postcode**

Registered Charity No. 00000000

Reply-paid envelope

You should enclose a reply-paid envelope: apply to your local Post Office for a licence. You can choose first or second class post. You will be given the number of pre-printed envelopes you require and you will have to overprint the address. You pay only for the replies you receive. Many charities now print on the envelopes that if the donor sticks on a stamp this avoids the charity having to pay for the cost of the reply.

The enclosures

Of course your letter will be as creative as you can make it, but you can also include imaginative enclosures to go with the letter. Direct mailshots get more and more ingenious and more and more expensive. But since the criteria for success are a good response rate and a good return on investment you can be sure that the more sophisticated users of the medium know what they are doing.

The Royal National Institute for the Blind (RNIB) recently mailed a small piece of cloudy plastic, which was obviously inexpensive, so that by looking through it addressees were able to 'see' for themselves the effect of impaired vision. A charity for the homeless mailed a sheet of newspaper just before Christmas, making the point that this was all that some people had to cover themselves with.
. . . .

Testing
. . . .

If you have an expensive idea such as mailing a fresh egg (goodness knows why!) you can test the concept by mailing just a few to see if you get a positive response. However, as the average response to a mailshot is about 1 per cent, your expensive gimmick has got to be outstanding to show any benefit on a test mailing of say 50 letters!

Let me quote two examples of successful enclosures used in the pioneering days of direct mail. The first involves the drug company selling a remedy for a nasal complaint which mailed every doctor in the country – rather a cynical lot because of a surfeit of mailings – with a freshly cut rose. As an attention-getter, a second company included in its mailing little boxes which were folded flat but jumped out of the package as a box.

Timing
. . . .

Timing is not important in isolation, but your mailshot could be more effective if it is linked to a significant national or local event such as Cup Final day, St George's day, Burns night or perhaps a local fair. Paradoxically, Christmas is a good time because people are feeling generous; summer-holiday time is not because people are either away or saving for holiday expenses.

Analysis

To learn about the effectiveness of a direct mailshot, it is crucial to analyse the responses you gained. These are some of the criteria to apply:

- total amount of money raised;
- percentage response rate;
- cost of the mailshot per reply received;
- average gift received;
- cost per £100 received.

If you can, analyse the donors by sex, home district, whether they have given previously and are on your database, whether they are members of a specific association, and so on. You could also test two different approaches and compare the results.

Constant analysis and feedback enable you to hone your operation so that direct mail – and indeed other techniques – become more and more cost-effective.

ADVANTAGES

- Local identity gives you a ready-made benefit.
- You might hit the jackpot with one extremely generous gift.
- You should get lots of names of potential supporters to add to your database.

DISADVANTAGES

- Mailshots can be expensive, although you can minimise the risk by pre-testing.
- Direct mailing is labour-intensive: if you do not sub-contract you will need lots of volunteers.
- You may lose the goodwill of important people if their mailing is doubled up.
- Direct mail can sometimes take one or two years to start making a profit.

RESOURCES

- If you have a patron who is a respected local figure, the letter could appear to come from him or her (although it will probably be written by you).
- If you have a computer with appropriate software and a colour printer you can produce the letter heading, letter and enclosures, and print them yourself.
- You will need lots of volunteers to stuff and label the envelopes.
- The Direct Marketing Association (see Appendix I) can help with free advice.

PUBLICITY

- You can support your direct mailing with your charity's ongoing posters, free mentions in local press and on radio.
- Link the mailing to an event.

KEY POINTS

- It is important to target your mailing precisely.
- You will be competing with many other mailshots.
- Be sure you have something worth saying.
- State clearly what the money is needed for.
- Longer letters with enclosures may work better.
- Always analyse the results.

CHAPTER SIX

Telephone appeals

Telephone selling – or, in the case of a charity, appealing – is exactly that: using the telephone to call a carefully selected list of prospects in order to make your pitch. Telephone sales is a technique used by many commercial organisations, such as those selling double glazing or new kitchens. For charities the telephone is a useful card to have up your sleeve: its prime use is for appeals, but it can also be used for selling tickets for events, or both.

Getting started

Reputation

There is no point even *considering* a telephone appeal if your charity is not known locally. (Chapter 16, Publicity techniques, explains how to go about ensuring that your charity is known even without spending any money.) Get going with your publicity before you get started with your telephone appeal. Your appeal will work best if you need the funds for an easily identifiable project.

The list

You will need a list of suitable telephone numbers; it is not cost-effective to plough through the telephone directory because most of the homes you ring will be totally unsuitable.

You can get a list of names, addresses and phone numbers of more well-to-do homes ('ABs' in marketing jargon), identified by their postcodes, from a company such as the Business Research Group (see Appendix I). This will cost you about £700 per thousand names – cost-effective if only a few people give you a large donation. And for this amount you could refine the list still further by specifying high net worth investors (people who own over a thousand shares in blue-chip companies) which would greatly increase the cost-effectiveness of the campaign. You can also get lists of young and affluent people: ideal perhaps if yours is a 'green' charity. You can order as few as 250 names.

Although you can pay for lists of contacts up to 30 days in arrears, many small local charities who have no money at all dare not take the risk even if the expense is justified. In this case you can go round to your local council offices and ask to see the electoral roll. You will have established from your research (Chapter 2) in which wards or branches the better-off people live. You can photocopy the lists and then look up the telephone numbers in your local phone book (bearing in mind that about 30 per cent will be ex-directory).

Another option is to seek out sponsorship for your campaign from a local business (see Chapter 9, Local business support, and Chapter 16, Publicity techniques).

Before you telephone people from your list, be sure to check their names against your list of regular donors and those who have granted your charity a legacy. In this way you can ensure that you do not appeal for a donation from people who already support you.

CASE NOTE
••••••••
A representative of a local charity called to ask for a donation from someone who was already a regular donor. The caller knew nothing of the substantial support that the donor was already giving to the charity. As a result, the charity lost the donor's annual gift, and a legacy.
••••••••

The script

. . . .

When making a telephone appeal, it is essential to work from a script which provides for various contingencies as the conversation progresses. Below is an example of a typical script (for a fictitious charity, Saved).

Good afternoon/evening, Mr/Ms/Mrs/Miss [name], I'm calling on behalf of Saved and I'm [caller's name]. Do you have a few minutes spare to talk to me?

Thank you. I'll be as brief as I can. Let me assure you I'm not going to ask for a donation.

Firstly, I'd like to thank you so much for the help you've given Saved – your support is vital in everything we do so thank you very much. I'm phoning you today about a new campaign we are launching to help protect our environment.

Mr/Mrs [name], some of our most valuable and beautiful wildlife is threatened because of the over-abstraction of water from our wetlands and rivers. Water companies are taking so much precious water from streams, rivers and wildlife sites that they are literally drying out. This endangers not only rare habitats like fens and chalk streams but also unique species like otters, water voles and fen orchids.

The outrage is that due to mismanagement, up to 20 per cent of the water you pay for could be leaking away because of badly maintained pipes.

That is why Saved is working both locally and nationally to put pressure on the government and water companies. We must force them to manage and regulate our water supplies and meet agreed conservation targets.

Mr/Mrs [name], to ensure we can keep this vital issue on the agenda, we need your help. We're aiming to raise £2 million to help save our natural habitats.

Testing

Before embarking on the campaign proper, test the script by telephoning a dozen or so names (or more if you do not have a clear result) in order to be sure that the script is working and does not need modifying.

Good practice

People and telephones

If you are a local charity (or even a branch of a national charity) you are unlikely to have sufficient 'spare' telephones or people to carry out the campaign after your test (see above). The least costly option is to arrange for volunteers to call from their own homes, after 6pm when calls are cheaper and the wage-earners are more likely to be back from work, but not after 9pm as this is illegal (see Appendix II).

There are organisations which train volunteers (some are listed in Appendix I). Students, and people with good voices who are both used to the public and resilient, make the best volunteers. The best method of finding such volunteers is through personal contact. Advertising and other methods often produce a lot of unsuitable candidates.

Volunteers need to know how to make contact, to build a relationship in seconds, how to make an appeal and how to close.

CASE NOTE

An Oxford University college, having telephone numbers of former students, asked current students to telephone with details of an appeal. There was an instant rapport between old and current students.

Control

If you can find a room which will take several telephones this is ideal, or you will have to monitor calls made from your volunteers' home. It is a legal requirement to monitor appeal calls, and your local BT office can advise you on this. You will need to produce a control form. This must state: the volunteer's name, the contact, their telephone number, the time of the call, any donation made, the method of payment, and any call back.

A credit-card donation is ideal, but for donations over £50 you must allow a cooling-off period of one week to give people time to reconsider.

A telephone bureau (see Appendix I) can do the telephoning and monitoring for you. Obviously this will be another extra cost but may be more cost-effective because only professionals are involved. A bureau will also write and test the script.

ADVANTAGES

- You are making a personal contact with your prospect and you have a local identity.
- Donations made by credit card are immediate.
- Telephone appealing can also be cost-effective. It may be possible to average raising about £60 per caller per hour (say from ten calls). However, with just one large donation you could have done very much better.

DISADVANTAGES

- The method is very labour-intensive, and up-front costs can be high if you do not have sponsorship.
- Some people may find unsolicited calls intrusive to the extent that you can lose their goodwill.

RESOURCES

- Suitably trained volunteers, or a bureau.
- A list of contacts (either bought, made up from your own records, or derived from the electoral roll).
- A good administration and control system.
- Good legal advice. (The Institute of Charity Fundraising Managers – see Appendix I – publishes a code of practice for telephone donations.)

PUBLICITY
··········
- Your charity must be known for a telephone appeal to be successful.

- Try to tie in your appeal with the local radio station and the local press.

KEY POINTS
··········
- Consider whether telephone appealing is likely to be cost-effective for your charity.

- Compile a list of telephone numbers to call from your own records, or research or buy one.

- Decide whether to use volunteers or a professional bureau.

- Be aware of the ethical and legal issues regarding use of the telephone (see Appendix II).

··········

CHAPTER SEVEN

House-to-house and street collections

House-to-house and street collections have been effective methods of fundraising for hundreds of years – mention is even made in the Bible of house-to-house collections. In this century, largely as a result of the increase in collections after the First World War by displaced demobilized soldiers looking to support themselves, legislation was introduced in 1939 and 1947 making it mandatory to have a council licence. For both house-to-house and street collections, indeed, procedures need to be followed rigorously in setting up, monitoring and concluding the collection.

House-to-house collections

The national charities arrange house-to-house collections in better-off areas by finding volunteers in each street who drop envelopes into 30–50 homes together with a leaflet about the charity, which also explains that the collector will call back in a few days to collect the envelope (which must be sealed for security reasons).

You could do the same thing for your charity, but as legislation stands at the moment, unless you have a Home Office exemption order, you must have special permission from the local police. (You can get a permit to collect from the local council but cannot use envelopes without police permission.) Collecting goods from door to door for sale in a charity shop also comes under the same law as collections of money, and a permit is similarly needed.

The best way of finding reliable volunteers is through local associations and your own supporters. When everything is planned like a military operation (it will take two to three months to do this), gather everybody together in a convenient place like a village hall, allocate the areas that they are going to collect and issue them with numbered collecting boxes. Alternatively, it may be more practicable to send out instructions and collecting materials by post. Records must be kept of each collection.

If your charity's bank agrees, the collectors (or you) should take the sealed envelopes to your charity's bank and have the envelopes opened and the money counted in their presence by the bank staff. For all but very small collections, most banks ask collectors to count the money themselves, in front of a witness, and either pay in a giro slip or send a cheque for the sum collected. Place the proceeds in a separate account to keep records distinct from those of other monies.

CASE NOTE
. . . .
A devoted volunteer wrote this letter on her own initiative with spectacular results. You could supply your collectors with a similar letter.

Dear Neighbour

I have undertaken to make a collection in our Close on behalf of the Grey Place Charity for young children. As you can see, some local high-profile people are helping to publicise this special anniversary year and the Duke [a local figure] is Patron of the Charity.

I know this sort of collection can be a nuisance and you may already be donating to other charities, but even some loose change from your pocket would be much appreciated, and every little helps.

I will come around for the envelope over the Bank Holiday weekend – or if it is easier you could drop it through my letter box (No. 12).

Many thanks for your help and support for this deserving cause.
. . . .

Street collections

········

Street collections are exactly that: collectors in the street holding a collection box decorated with your charity's name (perhaps even wearing a special outfit) and collecting money from passers-by. The term 'street collection' has been extended to cover collecting in supermarkets, shopping malls and even railway stations. There are a number of points to bear in mind.

- You must have a licence from the council. This is not easy to obtain and it is advisable to obtain one months in advance of the collection.

- Get all appropriate permissions in writing.

- Plan with military precision. Ideally you need two or three months' lead time.

- You will need to recruit a large number of volunteers; each volunteer must know exactly which is his or her pitch and the times at which they are to collect.

- Work on a session of one or two hours at a time for each collector.

- Boxes should be numbered and records kept of all amounts collected.

Collecting boxes should be opened and counted in front of witnesses and a return is required by the council. You could identify a local snack bar as a meeting place for refreshments and debriefing. This will help morale and prepare your collectors to 'smile' when they are back on duty again. 'Smiling' and catching the eye is all they are allowed to do. They must not rattle the boxes. There are other places where you may be able to collect such as at football matches and other large venues, but these are specialist in their requirements.

Alexandra Rose Day (ARD)

···········

National collections such as Alexandra Rose Day (see Appendix I) are well known. The Day was established by Queen Alexandra – the widow of Edward VII – in 1912. It is an umbrella organisation, and small charities are allocated specific areas in which to collect. They are supplied with collecting materials but must find their own collectors, and they keep a percentage of the proceeds. It is a great opportunity for the collectors to dress in Edwardian clothes with huge hats – a great motivator for them and the local press love it.

Counting the money

You will need a safe place to open collection boxes and count the money. Your bank might provide you with a room. You need two independent witnesses who have no direct contact with the charity to count the money with you. And when it is counted, place it on deposit in the charity's account.

Legal implications

The Charities Act 1961 (amended 1993) covers collections in depth, and some guidance is included in Appendix II. Current legislation is included in ICFM guidelines (see Appendix I). New legislation (Part III of the Charities Act) is currently being developed, but a date for the end of this process has not been specified at the time of writing (May 1997).

ADVANTAGES

- Collections will publicise your charity and raise money at the same time.
- They may also enable you to recruit long-term helpers.

DISADVANTAGES

- You will need lots of volunteers.
- Administration can be time-consuming.
- It is difficult to recruit reliable collectors.
- The cost of collecting materials can be high.

RESOURCES

- Collectors' kits of: letters, leaflets, badges and perhaps sashes.
- Bright collection boxes with a well-executed surface design.

- Lots of motivated volunteers.
- Full insurance.

PUBLICITY
....

- Attractive boxes will help promote your cause.
- Ideally, you should tie in with other local promotional activity.
- Posters everywhere will help to encourage people to donate.

KEY POINTS
....

- Collecting is one of the few techniques for core funding.
- There are many different types of collection so you must choose the one or ones which are right for you.
- You must comply with all legal requirements.
- Remember new legislation is pending.
- There are opportunities to recruit long-term volunteers and potential helpers.

....

Note in early 1988, *Running a Successful Public Collection* will be published by the Charities Aid Foundation.

CHAPTER EIGHT

Local newspaper and radio appeals

Local newspapers, paid for and free, together with local radio stations, have enormous coverage of their population in most areas – often more than the national newspapers and radio stations.

Newspapers

The local situation

The local press today is very complicated because of the mix of paid-for and free newspapers and the fact that many belong to a 'series' covering quite large areas. While they may appear as many different titles for local marketing purposes, many papers have editorial elements in common and only certain pages are exclusively dedicated to one area.

Where to find details of local press

The Newspaper Society (the trade association for the regional press – address in Appendix I) has a database of local free-sheets and paid-for newspapers. The BRAD Publishing Group publishes details of all media, including local newspapers. Their publications can be found in most large reference libraries.

Your own local newspapers will have the name of the editor and whether the paper is one of a series such as the *Recorder* series.

Who to contact

With a small paper you will deal directly with the editor. The
larger ones will have a news desk. Newspaper people are very
busy – have your story to hand. One conversation with the news
desk may mean that your press release is read (see Chapter 16,
Publicity techniques). Your charity may receive other coverage
if you send in articles from time to time about what your charity
is doing. Newspapers are always looking for photographs as well
as stories. Some of the larger ones may have a journalist who
specialises in local charities. If you are a branch of a national
charity you will have a press department which should be
able to help you obtain local press publicity.

Fundraising

Your local newspaper may give coverage about your charity and
include a donations slip. This is highly popular at certain times
of year (Christmas and Easter), but avoid the summer holiday
season. The Newspaper Society has lists of promotions which
involve the local press; sometimes a local business, such as a
supermarket or a large department store, is also involved.

CASE NOTE

A shopping centre's profits were low for various reasons. The
public relations officer approached a local charity. Together they
talked to several new companies moving into the area – new
members of the Chamber of Commerce. Through a joint
publicity and fundraising campaign, £7,000 was raised for the
charity in four hours of collecting.

- The local press gave a full-page report on the charity.

- The companies supported the report by advertising on the
  page.

- The newspaper ran a competition for readers to think of a
  slogan for each company. A charity donation form was
  included. (The paper also gave the charity plenty of coverage
  for several weeks before the promotion.)

- The shopping centre was the focus of a day's activity: a clown
  entertained children (one of the companies sold toys);

balloons were let off (the sender of the one going furthest received a prize); and a well-known celebrity wore an outstanding jumper made by one of the companies (a duplicate was also a prize). He made an appeal through the newspaper and on radio for the charity. Static collecting boxes were circulated to local shops and banks.

- The story was kept alive for several weeks through follow-up events and media coverage.

··········

Radio

··········

There may be several local radio stations covering your area: both BBC and commercial. The *Radio Authority Pocket Book* gives up-to-the-minute information (see Bibliography). BRAD and *The Major Companies Guide* also include details of local radio stations.

Who to contact

··········

The station manager is your main contact but individual presenters may also give you time between items or music. A member of your charity's client group, particularly someone who is grateful to your charity, will hold audiences, as will a charismatic chairperson. Often people do not want to contact a charity direct, so telephone helplines are always popular.

Effectiveness

··········

Local radio stations are less pressured than national stations. They rarely have a charity budget, but an appeal – especially by a local celebrity – can be most effective.

Advice and training

··········

The Directory of Social Change and Media Trust offer training in using the media (see Appendix I). Syndicate Services provides a news service for local charities, and the Community Radio Association is helpful. A copy of the Community Radio Act 1990 is a useful reference tool.

CASE NOTE

Local community groups and charities benefited from a £70,000 donation. This was made by a major nearby airport to celebrate its 50th birthday. The local press and radio asked readers to nominate local projects.

ADVANTAGES AND DISADVANTAGES

- Appeals in the local press and on radio can be used to good effect with other fundraising techniques – events, collections, direct mail, telephone appeals, legacy drives.

- This technique is inexpensive, and liked by patrons and celebrities.

- The main disadvantage is that it can be difficult to control the message published or broadcast.

RESOURCES

- Lots of energetic volunteers.

- Celebrities or charismatic personalities.

- Contacts with local media.

KEY POINTS

- 'News' stories on radio and in local papers are a cheap means of communication.

- It is essential to keep in touch with key figures at the paper or radio station.

- Journalists are often grateful for 'emergency' people who can supply a story.

CHAPTER NINE

Local business support

We have seen how you can raise money through events, direct mail, telephone appeals and collections. Local businesses can also be a splendid source of support: their owners are in business to make money so that they can enjoy a reasonable standard of living. Nevertheless they serve the public, and if they are successful they usually feel deep down that they owe it to the community to give back some of the money they have taken out. They are also very much aware of the importance of local goodwill.

Giving to charity is a caring but tax-effective way of returning some of a business's profits while at the same time enhancing its reputation not only in the community at large but equally, if not more importantly, among its own customers and staff.

Types of business

Independent retailers

There are many kinds of local business and many ways they can help. The archetypal local business is run by an independent retailer who may be a second- or even a third-generation shopkeeper on the same site. They are often pillars of the local church, members of the Chamber of Commerce, masons or school governors, and so can be approached in many ways. They are invaluable contacts because of the goodwill that their many connections can bring to your charity. Don't overlook local garages which might tie in a new car launch with your charity on their forecourt and in the press.

Local retailers will give cash donations, but they are more likely to give potentially more valuable gifts in kind (but not cars at a local level!). Your charity can raffle, sell or offer these as prizes. Some retailers – particularly the newer ones – are more inclined to give if they are approached semi-publicly at a Chamber of Commerce event. (Gifts in kind can be as tax-effective a way of giving as donations – see Appendix IV. This is also covered in Chapter 11, Donations.)

The person you should aim to contact in an independent local business is the owner, the senior partner or the managing director. If you have not managed to make a personal contact then telephone or send a fax. It is not always easy to get the top person, and you may be asked to write. The same letter-writing principles apply here as those discussed in Chapter 5 save that your letter can be more personalised than a general mailing.

Chain stores and service industries

Chain stores include shops such as Boots, Marks & Spencer, Littlewoods, Dorothy Perkins, Waterstones, WH Smith. (Booksellers have been known to arrange book signings and 'get to know' author evenings for a named charity.) The local manager can give small donations, up to £5,000, without needing to apply to head office.

Service industries include businesses such as petrol stations, gas, electricity companies and BT, banks and building societies. They may have independent budgets to support local charities, but if you are a branch of a national charity check with your head office that they do not already have an understanding at national level – it would not be politic to cut across this.

The person to contact in the case of a branch of a national company or a service industry is the local manager. Many companies are now members of Business in the Community, and endorse 'cause-related marketing' as being good for both charity and company.

There are other possible benefits which can stem from your contacts with local branches of national chains, including sponsorship, secondment and payroll giving.

Sponsorship

You may receive sponsorship support from local businesses. It is always worth asking for sponsorship of publications such as leaflets, collecting envelopes or annual reports.

Secondment

Sometimes you can benefit from a secondment, whereby experienced senior and middle managers – often people who are approaching retirement – can be 'loaned' to your charity (while still being paid by their employer) and you gain the business skills and experience of the secondee.

Increasingly popular is '100 hours' secondment – three weeks, if full-time. These schemes are popular with the secondees, who are often interested in widening their interests as they approach retirement, and sometimes they stay on with the charity after retirement to help as a volunteer.

Marks & Spencer are keen on seconding their junior managers as they see this as a way of enabling them to get to know the local community. You can find out more about secondment from: Action and Employment in the Community, the Grand Metropolitan Trust, and British Telecom (listed in Appendix I).

Payroll giving

As the name implies, this is a scheme whereby employees – usually from large companies – agree to have a small amount deducted from their wage or salary and given to a nominated charity (this is discussed in more detail in Chapter 11, Donations).

Public houses

Publicans know what is going on within the community. People often talk quite openly in pubs, and landlords and landladies are usually pro-charity and can offer very useful leads. If they have a function room they may offer it for your use cheaply or for nothing. Sometimes they will even arrange events such as darts matches in aid of your charity. Remember that they too are looking for mentions in the local press, and that they like events which increase their trade.

Talk to the publicans when they are not desperately busy: they may well allow you to collect directly from the customers providing that you do not pester them. Anyone collecting on a pub-to-pub basis must have a 'house-to-house' permit to do so (see Chapter 7).

CASE NOTE
· · · · · · · · ·
One charity run by nuns and working to alleviate poverty has a remarkable fundraiser. Sister Collette takes a collecting box to local public houses after football matches. The managers know the Order and the work it does locally. The Sister raises profile and serious money. Going to pubs alone to collect funds is not to be recommended, but they can be a source of core funding.
· · · · · · · · ·

National charities increasingly arrange tie-ups with breweries and if you are a branch of such a charity you should benefit enormously from the national publicity. Be aware, however, that some 'causes' do not lend themselves to association with breweries or tobacco companies. It is wise to check that any support does not clash with the ethos of the charity.

Professionals
· · · · · · · · · ·
Solicitors, accountants, estate agents (who can be chartered surveyors), bank managers and public relations consultants (listed in the *Yellow Pages* or *The Thomson Local* directory) are useful local contacts and possible sources of support.

Head offices
· · · · · · · · · ·
If the head office of a national or multi-national company is in your local area, this can be an excellent opportunity. Big companies almost always want to foster local relations. The

person to contact is the community relations officer, the public relations officer, or, if you plan a product tie-in, the marketing director – unless of course you have a personal lead to the chairperson, managing director or chief executive. (Even a relatively junior employee of a major company who is keen on your charity can be a good 'lead' for making a high-level contact.)

Closing

'Closing' is the marketing term for tying up a deal. If you succeed in making an appointment with any local business people, do prepare yourself well beforehand: know exactly what you are going to say, state precisely what you want from them (whether it is money or help), and what you can offer them in return. Try never to leave without an agreement. (One successful fundraiser advises that you should suggest an outrageous figure and, when your contact stops blinking, move in quickly and tie up the deal!)

When you have received a donation, thank the donor in person, and in writing. Keep in regular touch and let them know how your charity is developing (as businesspeople they will be interested), and call back again.

Associations

Chamber of Commerce

The 'Chamber' is the centre of local business life and a worthwhile source of contacts.

Many local businesses will be members, and the Chamber movement is now very active. There are regional groups as well, and the Chambers are barometers of the economic health of an area.

Junior Chambers, which you should make a point of joining if you are under 40, have dynamic members who actively enjoy taking part in the charity scene by raising money at social events. The business faculty of the local university is usually represented on the Chamber, offering training in career development and technological skills.

Freemasons

Members join the Masons through a specific 'lodge', often associated with a trade or profession. They are well known for raising money for charity, and the Masons often publish a local newsletter.

Other local groups

Other business groups which you should not neglect are: Business in the Community, the Community Development Foundation, the Local Enterprise Agency, and the Association for Business Sponsorship of the Arts (addresses in Appendix I).

You should make use of the *Chamber of Commerce Journal*, hopefully for a free mention, also the *Rotarian Journal* and the *Journal of Soroptimists* (the female equivalent of the Rotarians), and the Lions newsletter (The Lions organisation – and the young Lions, the Leos – are devoted to service to the community and are effective fundraisers). You will find more about these groups in Chapter 15, Other local organisations.

ADVANTAGES

- Your charity can achieve widespread support.
- You can achieve a spread of donations to suit different techniques.
- The business community is usually supportive of charities.

DISADVANTAGES

- Your charity or activity must fit in with supporters' business plans.
- You must stand out from all the other local charities.
- Initial contact can be difficult.

RESOURCES
. . . .

- Your own personality and contacts.

- A smart annual report and accounts, if you're an established charity; otherwise a clear, well-presented statement of your objectives, including why funding is essential.

- A video which you may be able to get produced for you free of charge by a local advertising agency, public relations company or college.

- A local celebrity – possibly your patron (as discussed in Chapter 2) – or celebrities. A distinguished patron will help to give you more authority.

PUBLICITY
. . . .

- Local businesses often share publicity budgets half and half with their suppliers who may well agree to your charity coming in.

- Many local businesses have close links with local radio and newspapers because of their own need for constant promotion and may agree to your charity sharing this publicity for free because of the goodwill that rubs off on both the advertiser and the media organisation.

- If your charity is not well known, local businesses are unlikely to respond to you.

- If you can afford it, use paid-for advertising, but try to get free mentions in county magazines, local newspapers and on local radio.

KEY POINTS
. . . .

- Different types of business require different approach techniques.

- National companies can provide extra benefits.

- Don't overlook local associations.

- Always go to meetings well prepared.

- Try never to leave a meeting without an agreement.

. . . .

CHAPTER TEN

Charity shops

Many of the major national charities such as OXFAM have shops in the high street where they sell secondhand goods, usually donated, to raise funds. There is no reason why your local charity cannot use the same technique. Because a charity does not have the start-up costs of a normal retailer it is possible to move into an empty site for as little as six months or less and still make money.

Setting up a shop

How to find a site

You may notice empty shops in the high street yourself and need to contact local estate agents or the Chamber of Commerce to find out if they are available – preferably for free or a peppercorn rent. These contacts may also have knowledge of sites becoming vacant before any notices to let appear. The ideal site would be in a busy area, possibly near other charity shops, but not too up-market.

Shop fittings and stock

Secondhand fixtures and fittings can be obtained from other shops. An advertisement in the local press can often bring good results. Charity shops should benefit from Council Tax exemption and tax relief (see Appendix IV).

Potential customers prefer charity shops which have a speciality such as bric-a-brac, secondhand clothing, books, or craft goods produced locally. You should decide what to sell. Encourage people to bring suitable goods along to the shop or arrange door-to-door collections.

Staff

You will need to recruit a manager – preferably a volunteer – who has had retail experience, and perhaps 20 or so helpers (also volunteers): sufficient to maintain a rota of part-timers.

Good contacts for recruiting helpers are the Women's Institute, the Townswomen's Guild, and local churches. Notices in the shop or in the local paper (free if you have cultivated the advertising manager!) can also help to find volunteers. Training is available (see Appendix I).

Keeping control

It is important that you have a business plan before you start running a shop, just as for any other business venture. Consider setting up a shop committee chaired by an accountant, a bank manager or an experienced retailer. If your charity has a head office it will probably have a shop controller who can provide guidelines.

Any agreement or lease should be carefully checked by a solicitor (your charity may retain one). Insurance cover should be arranged through a broker, whom if you have played your cards right you will have met through the Chamber of Commerce. The shop landlord may insist on specific requirements such as particular opening hours.

Running a charity shop requires good pricing, stock control and stock rotation, as with any other shop. It is also important to be aware of how to set out stock to limit pilfering. Turnover and costs must be constantly monitored to ensure that the shop is in profit, and a percentage of the profits should be set aside for project development. *The Charity Shop Handbook* published

by the Charities Advisory Trust (address in Appendix I)
is an essential reference tool.

ADVANTAGES
· · · · · · · · ·
- A charity shop in the high street will immediately raise the profile of your charity.
- It can act as a useful centre of information exchange.
- It can raise good profits from donated goods sold in a free or very low rental shop.

DISADVANTAGES
· · · · · · · · ·
- Running a shop can be risky, which is why you need experienced people behind you.
- Staff are not always easy to retain.
- You may find yourself having to vacate the premises at very short notice.

RESOURCES
· · · · · · · · ·
- An experienced retail manager.
- Lots of volunteers.
- Goods to sell.

PUBLICITY
· · · · · · · · ·
- Mentions on local radio and in local newspapers.
- Posters in libraries, supermarkets, public houses and other meeting places.
- Special events such as a fashion show or a children's reading.

KEY POINTS
· · · · · · · · ·
- A suitable shop site must be chosen.
- Rental arrangements must be agreed.
- Good financial controls are essential.
- A manager experienced in retail is essential.
- You must have a continuing supply of goods to sell.
- Constant promotion is important.
· · · · · · · · ·

CHAPTER ELEVEN

Donations

It is sometimes thought that donations are an entirely reactive form of fundraising: all you need do is wait for the gifts to arrive. That's not true at all, and, in practice, seeking donations is decidedly proactive. There is a great deal that you can do about making donations roll in. And they can come from a millionaire or the most humble wage-earner.

Big gifts, which by their very nature are unpredictable, can amount to half or even more of a charity's income. Routine donations which come through tried and tested formulas may seem more prosaic but are nevertheless important because the income is more predictable.

Types of gift

Big gifts

Soliciting big gifts is very much a function of the fundraising committee, which you can attend as an observer if you are an employee of the charity. The ball will start to roll if the chairperson or another member of the committee – or perhaps your patron – is able through their contacts to persuade a wealthy individual or their company to provide for a generous donation which can be promoted as the start of a fundraising drive. Committee members who are personally able to give a large gift, or directly to influence the giving of one, are obviously valuable to the charity, but such a source of income cannot be guaranteed.

The size of the gift will depend upon the wealth of the donor and the scale of the charity.

Some local charities may have annual budgets as small as £30,000 – some are even smaller – and some may have turnovers in excess of £500 million.

Even though you are looking to relatively high-powered committee members to bring in the big gifts it is an important discipline to have a donations plan which can be reviewed at your regular committee meetings.

The planning schedule, which must of course be highly confidential, could take this form (though you might decide that a different format is more appropriate for your charity):

PROSPECT	RESULT
WHO ASKS	FOLLOW-UP
MONTH	COMMENTS
TARGET AMOUNT	

You should also produce a donation kit for all your committee members, consisting of a personalised folder containing:

- a copy of the charity's annual report;
- a succinct statement of how much money is needed and how it will be used;
- benefit(s) to the donor (career advancement, a warm glow, social kudos);
- a specimen appeal letter (see Appendix III);
- publicity material;
- your latest newsletter.

CASE NOTE
....
It is worth considering unusual sources of donations. Local refuges and many victim support organisations receive assistance from police funds. The police service, and others working in the community, note those charities assisting locally.
....

Routine donations

This is the term used when a supporter gives a regular amount monthly, annually or sometimes even weekly. These provide the guaranteed regular income of the charity. If, as is usual, the routine donors greatly outnumber the big-gift givers, they are therefore a very important element of your funding base.

Keep your routine donors continuously informed of what is happening, and invite them to social occasions and events. (This is far easier to organise for a local charity than for a national one.)

The following are ways of giving tax-effective regular donations:

- Giftaid: a gift of £250 or more net of basic rate of tax. The charity can reclaim the basic rate of tax.

- Give As You Earn: a salaried or wage-earning employee on PAYE can agree to make donations through the tax system provided that their employer is a participant in the scheme.

- Deeds of covenant: a commitment to make a regular payment to a charity for at least four years.

- CAF voucher: the donor gives to the Charities Aid Foundation (CAF), listing those charities he or she wishes to support, and the amounts. CAF handles all the administration, including reclaiming the tax.

Appendix IV includes reviews of these four methods, and others.

'The ask'

A potential donor (or 'prospect') should be approached personally. The charity's representative may do this informally at a meeting or reception, or, if the prospect is a personal contact, a letter and supporting material may be sufficient.

The strength of local fundraising is the local network – hence the personal approach is best. For instance, one method found useful in church appeals is to take names from baptism, wedding and memorial service lists and invite keen members of the congregation at those services to ask for a donation. This also works well when current undergraduates ask graduates of their university for a gift for the church.

ADVANTAGES
- Big gifts, while not predictable, can be huge.
- Routine donations provide the backbone of the charity's income.
- Tax benefits can increase the income from some forms of giving.

DISADVANTAGES
- It can be difficult to motivate people to give.
- Big gifts can take time to materialise (or may never do so).
- Total income from donations is unpredictable.

RESOURCES
- Skilled help for researching and identifying potential donors.
- A celebrity to sign an appeal letter.

PUBLICITY
- Editorial mentions in quality press.
- Regular newsletters.
- A well-produced annual report.
- High-profile networking.

KEY POINTS
- Big gifts can be huge but are not predictable.
- The fundraising committee plays a key role.
- Routine gifts are the backbone of the charity's income.
- An 'appeal kit' can be useful for committee members.

CHAPTER TWELVE

Legacies

People leave money to charity for many reasons: very wealthy people sometimes create charitable trusts (discussed in Chapter 14); some people believe that they have left sufficient to their family and friends and prefer to give the rest to charity but don't always know which one; others want to say 'thank you' to a charity which has helped either themselves or a close relative. Women especially are living longer, often quite frugally, and tend to accumulate savings. Two-thirds of all charitable bequests are made by women.

Legacies do not just happen, and the national charities take them very seriously: some large charities raise half of their total income from legacies. Local charities tend to overlook this potentially huge source of income which requires a high level of interpersonal skills and diplomacy. However, it does depend very much on your locality and the nature of your charity whether you should devote time and effort to chasing what can be an unknown return. If you are based in a town where there are many retired folk and your charity helps older people then the effort would be well worthwhile.

There are professionals who can help to plan and co-ordinate your legacy activities. A discretionary wills service which monitors all grants of probate and informs subscribing charities when money has been left for charitable purposes at the discretion of executors is available both nationally and locally at a starting fee of £90. If such a case arises the charity would contact the executors and make their case (see Appendix I for addresses).

People who influence decisions

Solicitors

Even in these days of will forms and non-qualified will-writers, solicitors are still the most important people to court. They are the ones who are most often asked by their clients – who are usually the better off – to recommend a charity. They can also give advice about the different types of bequest:

- A pecuniary legacy, where the will contains a cash gift to someone or perhaps a charity.

- A specific bequest of an item: a car or a piece of jewellery, for example.

- A residuary legacy is what is left after the pecuniary legacies, specific bequests, debts, expenses and any tax have been paid. This can be good for charities because there is usually more left than most makers of wills realise in their lifetime.

- A reversionary, or life interest, is when someone leaves a house, for example, to a relative for his or her lifetime and after that relative's death it reverts to a beneficiary such as a charity.

Solicitors tend to be influential members of the community – often members of the Chamber of Commerce – so it is important for your charity to keep in touch with them.

Bank managers and chartered accountants

Elderly and wealthy people often discuss their will and financial matters with their bank manager or their accountant; once again you must be sure that these professionals always have your charity in the front of their mind.

Celebrities

A celebrity can sign your letters and give a testimonial in your legacy leaflet (see below).

Religious representatives

It is always a good idea to ensure that you and your charity have excellent relations with all the local religious organisations, and that they are supplied with literature about the charity and the names of local solicitors best disposed towards your charity.

Funeral directors

Funeral directors can also influence bequests because mourners sometimes ask if they can donate to a charity instead of sending flowers. Again make sure that local firms know all about your charity.

Bereaved families

If the family places an obituary notice in the local press suggesting a donation to charity instead of flowers, tactfully suggest that the donations be sent directly to the family for forwarding to the charity. The mourners are likely to be more generous if the family knows how much they have given.

People who know older people

This suggests virtually everybody, but in practice associations like the Chamber of Commerce, Rotarians and Soroptimists are more likely to be supported by 'caring' people. Here again, talks, and leaving your leaflet, can be a worthwhile investment. If yours is a branch of a national charity you will almost certainly have appropriate literature already.

You should provide all those people who influence decisions with your legacy leaflet. (Advice about how you might produce a leaflet is covered in Chapter 16, Publicity techniques.) Also, in order to keep your charity's name before the professional advisers, you could leave them with a small, personalised desk-top gift such as a pen, a diary or a memo pad which can be purchased from a specialist charity supplier who can provide you with a catalogue of options (see Appendix I).

Direct targeting

Older people

Obviously, it is not a good idea to march up to an older person and ask them point blank to make a bequest to your charity. The approach must be far more subtle. You can give talks about your charity's activities in day clubs, libraries and other places used by older people, and leave copies of your leaflet.

People within your charity

Don't overlook your own committee members and volunteers. Here again you cannot bludgeon them with requests to leave money to the charity, but you can discreetly enquire whether they have made a will, tell them how important it is that they should, and perhaps offer a will-making guide such as the one produced by Age Concern (address in Appendix 1).

Some of your charity's older members or volunteers, who are loyal supporters of the charity, might even appreciate a tactful reminder about a legacy.

Incidentally, it is a good idea to brief a fundraiser or volunteer to keep in touch with your committed legators and to advise them on any will-making problems. Specialist training on face-to-face interviewing for legacies is now available (see Appendix I).

Database of donors

You will have a database of people who have given to your charity. Once again you can hardly approach them directly, but an oblique approach asking several questions can be productive. For example, you could ask whether they would like to subscribe to a newsletter, if they would like to make a covenant (see Appendix IV) and whether they would like information on making a legacy.

Beneficiaries of your charity

The beneficiaries of your charity – in particular patients at hospices – may want to leave money to the charity and would even appreciate a reminder and perhaps an introduction to a caring solicitor who might be on your committee.

A solicitor on your fundraising committee might be prepared to provide a 'free' service to a potential legator in return for a bequest to the charity. If you do not have a solicitor, an excellent response letter (drafted by a professional adviser) to someone who has expressed an interest in leaving a legacy to a charity is included in Appendix III.

CASE NOTES

One charity was left a large sum by a woman who heard a talk by the Vicar at the local Women's Institute; the beneficiary was also inspired by the prospect of being able to watch the charity's garden for disabled people being built.

A solicitor tells of a client who left a considerable sum to a charity because the patron had the same surname as herself – and she liked his garden!

A man left a piece of paper as a will with the words 'For Mother'. Nobody knew whether this was intended to mean his mother or his wife.

ADVANTAGES

- Legacy fundraising can generate potentially large sums of money.
- It helps to build your charity's database, and may also encourage people to give before they die.

DISADVANTAGES

- Timing of income gathered from legacies is unpredictable.
- Legacy fundraising is only suitable for certain charities.

RESOURCES

- A solicitor or legal expert to advise you.
- Time to keep in touch with solicitors and other contacts.
- A specially trained fundraiser or volunteer to look after prospective legators.
- Database of supporters.
- Legacy leaflet.

PUBLICITY

- Celebrity endorsement.
- Advertising in specialist magazines.
- Talks to Chamber of Commerce, 50+ clubs and other gatherings.
- Posters which must be very discreet.
- Legacy leaflet.
- Reminder gifts for solicitors, bank managers and other key professionals.

KEY POINTS

- Are legacies relevant for your charity?
- You should have a legacy leaflet.
- Contact all the people who influence decisions.
- Any direct approach must be very tactful.
- Provide ongoing services to pledged legators, if requested.

CHAPTER THIRTEEN

Local authorities and health authorities

Local authorities give grants and contracts to local charities for particular projects. These are usually for local use for residents within the council area. County council health authorities also have limited funds for local health-related projects such as drugs education and services for drug users. Taken together these can be one of your charity's most important sources of funding and must be taken very seriously.

Sources of funds and whom to approach

The local authority has responsibility for education, transport, housing, leisure, social services, community services and technical services. Each interest has its own committee which may allocate grants. All local authorities also have dedicated grant departments. The finance director knows what funds are available and can be a useful ally. Political pressure affects all action and discreet lobbying of interested counsellors can also be worthwhile.

Health authorities have similar structures but are concerned with only health-related projects. The most appropriate person to court is usually the secretary. Occasionally parish councils may have funds available for projects.

CASE NOTE
· · · · · · · · ·
A local councillor had a child with learning difficulties who was placed in employment with the help of a local charity. The councillor was so impressed with the positive changes in his daughter that he helped the charity to apply for funds to the local authority. This interest and support led in turn to European funding as well.
· · · · · · · · ·

Types of funding
· · · · · · · · ·
Grants
· · · · · · · · · ·
Local authorities give grants for projects sometimes for two or three years. These are usually cash grants but can take the form of office space or goods in kind.

CASE NOTE
· · · · · · · · ·
The London Borough of Hounslow donated a Lancaster boiler from an old Victorian bath house to Kew Bridge Steam Museum.
· · · · · · · · ·

Contracts
· · · · · · · · · ·
Increasingly, local authorities, but not health authorities, are entering into contractual relationships with charities. This means that, in return for a regular payment, your charity must provide a specific service such as transporting older people to hospital. Terms and conditions have to be negotiated between charity and local authority.

You should have a copy of the NHS and Community Care Act 1990 which obliges statutory authorities to have a contractual relationship with relevant organisations. *Getting Ready for Contracts* and *Finance for Contracts* (see Bibliography) go into this in depth.

Joint funding
· · · · · · · · · ·
A local authority and a health authority can combine to support a charity – usually a 'start-up' – for just one year. The link between the two authorities is usually via their own senior

staff but you may have to present your charity's case to the joint consultants committee.

ADVANTAGES
. . . .
- Local authorities (but not health authorities) may support appeals which are not obviously popular but nevertheless of use to the community, such as helping people with learning difficulties or physical disabilities.
- They give worthwhile amounts over time – one of your best shots!
- Their support often encourages other potential funders such as trusts.

DISADVANTAGES
. . . .
- There are often very strict restraints on how the money can be spent.
- Apart from engaging in joint funding, local authorities are not keen on supporting brand-new charities.

RESOURCES
. . . .
- A senior spokesperson with knowledge of the 'system' who can lobby grant officers and council members.
- Ability to complete complex application forms and write detailed submissions.
- A specialist medical expert for health authority submissions.

PUBLICITY
. . . .
- Well-produced annual report and accounts.
- A video if you have one.
- Networking with the local Mayor, finance director and council members.

KEY POINTS
. . . .
- Potentially one of your most important sources of funding.
- Grants can be for cash or goods in kind.
- Increasingly, local authorities are entering into contractual relationships with charities.
. . . .

CHAPTER FOURTEEN

Trusts

Trusts, from the largest grant-making trust to the smallest local trust, are a major source of support and finance throughout the voluntary sector. Many are charities themselves – and they are an essential part of local fundraising.

Unlike most other potential sources of funds, trusts exist expressly to give away money, but the Trustees have to be satisfied that it will be put to good use. You need to establish excellent personal relations with the local trust 'correspondent' or 'secretary' (alternative terms). Some smaller trusts are administered by a local firm of solicitors or accountants, which can make personal contact more difficult.

One of the more interesting and potentially rewarding aspects of raising money from trusts can be tracking them down. Some local trusts are hundreds of years old and were set up on the death of landed gentry or merchants making specific endowments.

There can be quite a lot of money in small local trusts which can be put to the use of your charity if you find such a trust and approach it professionally, and if the endowment is appropriate. There is no point, for example, in applying to a trust set up to provide alms houses for the old men of the parish if your charity is for orphaned children!

Types of trust

Grant-making trusts

Although all trusts are grant-making, only the national ones are usually referred to as grant-making trusts. Grant-making trusts are usually huge charitable trust funds set up under the terms of a large estate by families such as Cadbury, Gulbenkian, Rowntree or Lever.

Local trusts

There are many types of local trust, one or more of which could be appropriate for the needs of your charity if you can track it down. They can be:

- tied to a locality or even a parish;
- for a specific need;
- a local company trust (see under Company trusts below);
- an endowment linked to a craft trade which may now have vanished (such as spinners or candle-makers).

Some local trusts will sometimes do their own research in order to find a charity to support – so you could be lucky!

Company trusts

Corporate trusts are funded by regular transfers of cash from a company.

Endowed trusts are formed by companies when they are doing well by setting aside money into a trust, completely separate from the company, by a 'one-off' transfer of assets. The trust can then spend the income generated. The Guinness Trust is an example which was not affected by the company being taken over by Distillers.

Staff funds refer to company trusts where the income comes from staff contributions, usually raised locally for a one-off appeal; however, sometimes the company may match the staff contributions or continue giving even after the original objective has been achieved.

Specific funds such as the BP Education Fund which you can approach if your charity's need is appropriate.

CASE NOTE
· · · · · · · · ·
The Allied Dunbar Staff Charity Fund is managed entirely by staff volunteers, organised into committees which visit projects and assess grant requests under three policy headings: independent living, crisis support, and children and young people. In addition, the Staff Charity Fund has an overseas committee which makes grants to projects in developing countries. The Staff Charity Fund's income comes from Deeds of Covenant made by 40 per cent of the 2,500 staff at the company's Swindon headquarters, a number of fundraising events and other activities. The company's charitable trust contributes a sum matching that raised by the staff.
· · · · · · · · ·

If you approach a company trust you should know whether the gift is conditional; for example, does a new piece of equipment have to carry the company name? In general, most trusts do not like publicity about their support, although company trusts may be the exception here.

How to find trusts

Reference sources

Fortunately, there are a number of excellent reference books which can help you in your search to find the right trust:

- *Directory of Grant-Making Trusts*, published by the Charities Aid Foundation, gives summary information about over 2,000 trusts including some of the larger local trusts.

- *Guide to the Major Trusts, Volume 1*, published by The Directory of Social Change, is a guide to the top 300 trusts.

- *Guide to the Major Trusts, Volume 2* covers the next 700 trusts including a few local trusts.

- Various regional grants guides are also published by The Directory of Social Change, but the *Yellow Pages* or *The Thomson Local* directory, under Charitable Organisations, often publish listings.

Details of these and other relevant publications are included in the Bibliography.

Other sources

The current Charities Act requires the Charities Commission to supply two copies of the listings of local charities on its index – many of which will be trusts – to the appropriate county and district authority every year. You can contact the finance director of your county or district who should help you to track down the trusts among the charities.

CASE NOTE

A local solicitor once turned down a grant application to a 'known' trust which he managed. However, he gave the charity seeking funds a cheque for £2,000 from a privately administered 'unknown' trust which he also managed. The charity was never told who the benefactor was!

Other sources include the following:

- Old established firms of solicitors and accountants often have knowledge of local trusts, some of which they manage themselves.

- Members of the clergy may also know about 'hidden' trusts in their parishes.

- Bank managers can be helpful with information about recently established trusts.

- Local newspapers report on large estates, particularly where money has been left for charitable purposes.

- Some national charities have knowledge of local trusts which may be helpful for local charities.

- The bi-monthly *Trust Monitor* published by the Directory of Social Change can be useful because it gives information on trust development and new trusts.

- The charity trade press often contains nuggets of information not published elsewhere.

- Your local Voluntary Services Organisation (VSO) may also provide information.

- The Charity Information Bureau, Councils for Voluntary Service, Rural Community Service, and, in Wales, Scotland and Northern Ireland, The Council for Voluntary Action, can also help with your search.

Funderfinder

Many local Councils for Voluntary Service have installed a computer program called *Funderfinder*, which sprang out of the West Yorkshire Information Bureau. It enables you to track down the most appropriate trusts to approach for funding for your charity. You fill in a detailed form giving a lot of information about your charity and the appeal. When this is run through the program, *Funderfinder* will make a 'shortlist' of trusts worth approaching. This could run into hundreds or be as few as half a dozen. The more carefully and accurately you complete the *Funderfinder* form, the shorter and more potentially rewarding your shortlist will be. When a shortlist is identified, it is then still necessary to look up each trust in the relevant publication to find all the other necessary details.

Planning and strategy

The short shortlist

Once you have identified the trusts most likely to be in sympathy with your charity, unless you have been very ruthless in your shortlisting, you may still be faced with a formidable number of trusts. Ideally you should shorten this list to one, but in reality you may have a list of three or more.

The first consideration is whether you, or any of your committee members, volunteers or contacts, know, or have any connection with, the secretary/correspondent (or perhaps the chairperson of the Trustees) of any of your shortlisted trusts. If you can make your first contact on a personal basis you will have a helpful start. Your contact may for example suggest the best time of year to apply and the ideal way to prepare your application.

If one of the shortlisted trusts has a strong association with the aims and objectives of your charity you might feel that this is the criterion to which you should give priority.

The approach

Telephone the secretary/correspondent, explain who you are, tell him or her about your charity, why you need funds and that you plan to approach their trust. Ask if you can meet – ideally at your offices – where you can explain your need more precisely and ask for advice about how you should pitch your application.

The secretary or correspondent may then give you helpful guidance. They would not be solely responsible for decisions to allocate grants, but would carry weight with the Trustees. What local trusts look for – quite apart from a worthwhile cause – is soundness and respectability, and they are often impressed if you have matching funds lined up.

Be warned: local trusts in particular will give grants for projects, but do not expect them to cover running costs.

The application

Even if you have not met the secretary or correspondent in person, telephone first and send your application in draft for initial comments.

Your letter asking for a grant should state briefly:

- whether the trust has supported you in the past;
- who you are and what you do;
- a brief history of your charity;
- how much you need and precisely what you intend to do with the money;
- what might happen if you don't get extra funding;
- what funding you already have, and the sources;
- any time constraints;
- whether any work is actually in hand or when you propose to do it, including names of any contractors who have been appointed or approached (if applicable).

Enclose a list of the supporting material (see below) you will be sending with the formal application, which in the event may be on a form supplied by the trust.

Having received back your draft letter from the secretary or correspondent with their comments, only then should you write formally sending the supporting material. (A specimen letter is included in Appendix III.)

Supporting material

You should send as much as possible of the following supporting material directly to the secretary/correspondent for safekeeping:

- a smartly produced annual report and accounts;
- your latest newsletter and previous copies if relevant to your application;
- a video if you have one;
- your existing publicity material;
- any press cuttings supporting your cause;
- details of senior staff with appropriate skills and experience;
- a detailed budget breaking down all the component parts of the project;
- a copy of your charity's constitution.

Note, however, that some trusts prefer to receive only a letter, a budget and an annual report initially, and will request other information if needed.

Multiple applications

You can approach more than one trust at a time, but, if asked, you must be honest about this. If you should receive more than one grant for a specific need then you must tell both (or all) of the trusts involved and either return the money or arrange a larger project.

ADVANTAGES
- Local trusts in particular are usually well disposed towards local charities.

- They can and often do fund whole or major parts of large projects.

- Many correspondents/secretaries are very helpful and will give advice.

DISADVANTAGES

- Trusts are sometimes reticent about giving all their criteria for making a grant.

- Trustees meet infrequently and sometimes do not let you know if your application has not been successful.

- Your application may require very detailed and time-consuming input and research which can be out of proportion to the amount received.

- Any grant you receive may not cover running costs.

RESOURCES

- Access to reference books on grant-making.

- Access to the *Funderfinder* program if your local council does not have it.

- The ability to write a good application letter.

- Time to research all the potential trusts thoroughly before making your first approach.

PUBLICITY

- Ongoing public relations and promotional activity.

- Secretary/correspondent and Trustees are aware of your charity before you make contact.

KEY POINTS

- Personal contacts are valuable.

- Trusts are a very important potential source of funding.

- Your own interpersonal and presentational skills will be tested.

- Sometimes your detective abilities are important to seek out the appropriate trust.

- The trusts want to help and will give you useful guidance.

- Applicants should have impeccable credentials.

CHAPTER FIFTEEN

Other local organisations

The key to local fundraising is networking. It will be easier to raise good sums of money if your charity is a 'part' of the local community.

Types of organisation

Social associations

Social associations may have a background of business, but exist for members to meet each other. They include:

- Rotary clubs (for business/professional men);
- Soroptimist groups (women's rotary);
- Chamber of Commerce and the Junior Chamber;
- The Lions and Young Lions;
- Round Table (business and professional people).

Local organisations often require speakers for their meetings, and this is a good way to introduce your charity to the group.

Women's organisations

Townswomen's Guilds and Women's Institutes are good sources of excellent volunteers but are less likely to want to fundraise for other organisations. It is worth keeping the secretaries informed about your activities.

Leisure activities and clubs

Leisure centres sometimes stage events for charity, for example a sponsored run or sponsored swim. Sometimes – especially if one of your staff, committee or volunteers is a member – a golf or tennis club might be interested in a sponsored event tied in with the local media. Bridge clubs might also arrange events on your charity's behalf. Local organisations such as golf, squash or bridge clubs 'adopt' a charity for a year, and will run events to raise funds for them.

Community services

Transport facilities (such as bus garages and railway stations), ambulance stations, the local fire and police stations will often take part in or organise fundraising events for a charity. As individuals the officers are also respected members of the community and will engender much goodwill for your cause. Sometimes the police give grants from their lost goods or 'unclaimed stolen goods' funds.

Educational establishments

Further education colleges and universities arrange 'rag days' which raise money for charity – and they prefer local charities in which they can become involved. The ebullience of some students may upset your committee members, however. One bright spark did a 'parachute drop in the nude', shaking an established charity to the core.

Most schoolchildren love being involved with a charity they know locally. If they can see the project for which funds are being raised then they will happily collect stamps or milk-bottle tops or write histories of the locality to sell in aid of your charity. Your initial approach should be made to the head teacher.

The right contacts

You can find details of local organisations in the *Yellow Pages*. If not, the reference section of your local library should have details of local organisations including the name of either the secretary or the chairperson. It is advisable to make contact with the head of local community services.

How to approach

The best way to make contact with a local organisation is through a 'warm' contact – someone you already know or have some connection with. If you cannot do this then a clergyman, Mason or Chamber of Commerce should be able to give a lead.

If all else fails, you can telephone the secretary to the association. You will be asked to put your proposal in writing, together with details of your charity – and with the letter you will need your annual report and other supporting material (including a video, if possible).

When to approach

The planning committees of most organisations meet in May to prepare the programme of events for the following autumn–spring. Your charity will be considered sympathetically if your work is recognised by members.

What local associations can do for you

As a very general guide:

- The Lions, Junior Chamber of Commerce and local community services become involved with local carnivals, fetes and other community events and will donate funds raised to your charity. They may arrange fundraising events for you.

- The Rotarians, Soroptimists and Round Table will ask for presentations.

If a group organises an event for your charity, do offer to help, for example by obtaining gifts for a tombola. And, if possible, always try to attend the event. Do say thank you to everyone involved in a fundraising event, and make a point of acknowledging their donated time and efforts.

Sometimes you will be given the opportunity of speaking – occasionally with little prior warning. If funds are raised, do offer a receipt and take the cash or cheque with you. Try never to leave empty handed – goodwill whittles away very quickly.

CASE NOTES

The chairperson of a business luncheon was startled when the Royal patron of a charity thanked the organisation for the generous amount raised by a raffle held during the proceedings and asked to be given a cheque there and then, and left with it in her handbag.

A women's organisation once raised considerable funds for a local charity, and nobody from the charity came to receive the cheque. The organisation continues to raise funds but for other charities.

ADVANTAGE

- Your charity joins the community network – which can be very loyal.

DISADVANTAGES

- Local organisations may often be already committed to specific charities.
- Sometimes a certain amount of lethargy needs to be overcome.
- Members of local groups may need to be persuaded of how they will benefit from working for your charity.

RESOURCES

- A good 'closer' (somebody who securely ties up a commitment to fundraising).
- A charismatic personality for giving presentations.

PUBLICITY

- Local organisations give to charities they know.
- Regular mention on local radio, in newspapers and county magazines.
- A presence at local events such as county shows and twinning with European towns.

KEY POINTS

- Being part of the local network helps raise funds and the profile of your charity.
- Keep in touch with members of local organisations.
- Networking yourself at receptions and other gatherings will keep your charity's profile high.
- Maintain, at all times, a good level of publicity.

CHAPTER SIXTEEN

Publicity techniques

Public awareness of your charity is essential for fundraising, and maintaining awareness can be easier for a local organisation than a national body. This chapter offers guidance on getting as much publicity as possible for your charity, mostly without paying for it, by using public relations techniques.

There are two golden rules: the first is that you are the custodian of a 'brand' whose identity and uniqueness you must protect tenaciously; the second rule is never be boring.

Having agreed the basic visual style of your organisation and your logo, it is important to keep to it so that it is easily recognisable. CAF, for example, is known throughout the voluntary sector.

Legal requirements for publicity materials are covered by Part II of the Charities Act (see Appendix II).

Types of publicity material

News releases

The information you send through to newspaper editors or radio station managers should be in the form of news releases or press releases. These should be delivered preferably by hand or faxed when the story is most newsworthy. Sometimes it is worth informing the press of forthcoming attractions, such as a Royal visit, and filling in the details later via the news release. Photographs are always appreciated. It does no harm to follow up a release with a phone call to the news desks to confirm interest.

The news release should have a clear and memorable headline such as 'Helping people find their way in an uncaring world'. Your story must be told simply and precisely, giving any venue, dates and names (as appropriate) as well as a contact name and telephone number. Do make sure that there is always somebody to answer journalists' questions – a home number if necessary as they often work well into the night. Fax numbers are always useful as journalists may need facts agreed or clarified. The date of the release must always be included.

The release should be typed double-spaced on your charity's letterhead and boldly titled PRESS RELEASE or NEWS RELEASE.

Sometimes it is necessary to issue a news release before the story is ready to break (if a garbled story is being circulated for example). In this case, mark the release with an 'embargo' date in the hope that the story will appear when you want it to, but remember it is not unknown for publications to break embargoes.

Chairpersons of charity committees are often keen to be featured in a radio interview or to give their views to the press. If your story is of specialist interest you may wish to contact a specialist publication or a particular journalist. Ensure that you provide plenty of information about your charity, but be careful not to overload your contact, and always keep the information interesting.

Cable television stations are often actively seeking local interest items to include in news and magazine programmes, and may be pleased to hear about your charity generally, as well as special events coming up.

The Internet

There are various organisations which can help charities to become connected to the Internet. (Details are included in Appendix I.)

CASE NOTE

One charity received a considerable sum through being on the Internet. A young man in Australia saw their appeal on his computer. He immediately sent a large cheque because the charity was benefiting his childhood village in the UK.

Annual report

Your annual report, which has so many uses other than being a legal requirement, does not have to be just a few pages of financial tables, although these should be well presented. It is also an opportunity for your chairperson, and possibly you as fundraiser, to write upbeat reports about your activities. You should send copies to your patron, committee members, volunteers, the media and your major supporters (with appropriate covering letters).

Newsletters

Another means of keeping in touch with potential funders is by regular newsletter. Funders always like to hear success stories and case histories of what has been achieved with the use of their own and other funds. Newsletters can also be a useful way to let your supporters know of developments without appearing to ask for funds.

Supporters can be encouraged to play an active role by sending in stories, photographs or letters. Newspapers are also useful for including inserts and for merchandising. Computer packages for presenting information in newsletter format are widely available, and you could aim to meet production costs by sponsorship or advertising. Asking volunteers to deliver newsletters by hand saves money and can help to build bridges with readers, giving the necessary human touch.

Posters

Posters may be produced in-house or with the aid of talented volunteers, perhaps from schools or art colleges. Commercial poster sites sometimes remain empty and you can offer to fill them for free. If this does not work, ask a local company to sponsor your campaign – keep the message simple but argue the benefits to the community from your charity's presence.

Smaller posters or handbills can be produced simply on a computer. When you have a supply ask a volunteer to walk into shops, pubs, cinemas and any other venues and ask if they will display your poster.

Leaflets

You will need a general information leaflet for your charity, and possibly specialist leaflets giving details of particular projects or requirements such as legacies. Again, there are appropriate computer packages available. Illustrations help to build a picture, and catching the imagination encourages people to give to your charity. An A4 sheet divided into three, making six sides, is ideal, and could include a side each with the following:

- your charity name, address and other contact details, an illustration and strong headline;
- a message from the patron;
- general information about the charity;
- information on particular projects;
- a donations form.

A personal computer with appropriate software, and access to a colour printer, will enable you to print several hundred copies of a leaflet – probably sufficient for a local charity. It's always useful to store artwork on computer for future use or adaptation.

It is a good idea to collect and study leaflets produced by the national charities as well as by the local competition.

Legacy leaflets

Some special points need to be noted when preparing a leaflet on legacies:

- Do not use legal jargon but remember that legacies are legal documents and so show a draft leaflet to a solicitor.
- Emphasise that your charity is local, and that leaving a legacy could ensure local remembrance that is more than just a name in a book or remembrance list.
- Give examples of legacies already left to your charity and say how useful they were.
- Include details of your legacy adviser and how to contact them.
- Include a section for further action, such as a pledge form.
- Celebrity endorsement carries a great deal of weight with potential legators.

Videos

Videos add interest to a presentation or back-up to printed material. They are expensive to produce, but a local college may produce one for you for free or expenses only. Scripting and tight editing is essential: it can be very useful if anyone connected with your charity has relevant professional experience.

Advertising

Local fundraisers tend to overlook advertising in the local press, but this can be a useful technique (see also Chapter 8, Local newspaper and radio appeals).

Your best contact is the display advertisement manager, who will not only have all the possible facts and figures to hand, but will know the local companies – their budgets, when they advertise and where, and if there is a chance that they would sponsor your advertisements.

Negotiating payment

All newspapers have a rate card showing the cost of advertising space. These are usually per page, half page, quarter page and eighth of a page. Many newspapers have charity rates. Before discussing discounts you will need to give your registered charity number.

It is worth having an advertisement always to hand as 'spots' sometimes need filling – you may even obtain free space this way. If you have a good relationship with the advertising sales team they may give you contacts within local companies who advertise and may sponsor your advertisements. The telesales team may be willing to make contact for you otherwise you will need volunteers to approach likely companies.

The advertisement

It is helpful to know the newspaper and series and also to watch the national newspapers to see how the large charities advertise. The latter will have the support of specialised creative agencies.

These are the basic principles for an advertisement:

- Be clear about the purpose of the advertisement.
- Include a good heading or strapline.
- Specify any action to be taken as a result of reading the advertisement, for example leaving money to the charity, attending an event, becoming a volunteer or giving a donation.

Inviting donations

The most effective method of obtaining funds from an advertisement is with a donations form. (A suggested response coupon is shown in Chapter 5, Direct mail.) As your charity is local, donors prefer to respond to somebody they know and trust who lives locally. Many people will call in person to leave a donation, as they like making direct contact. Make sure you record these donations accurately, so that responses can be monitored. Always check that the costs of advertising are covered by the income. You may consider a freepost address or freephone telephone number, and will need to discuss these with the post office or BT/Mercury.

All advertisements are covered by the Code of Advertising Practice administered by the Advertising Standards Authority (address in Appendix II).

Legacy advertising

Small-coupon advertising for legacies has proved to be effective for some charities. There are two approaches: targeting the general public directly, and focusing on professionals such as solicitors. You may be able to tie in with discreet professional advertising. Again, emphasise the local connection strongly, suggesting that people leaving you money will have a close connection with you and will be able to see how the charity progresses.

Using professionals

If you have a public relations agency and advertising agency in the business community it is worth suggesting that they form a connection with you as 'their' charity. The agency will gain goodwill and opportunities to show their creativity. You will have a professional campaign – preferably for free. The agencies may have wealthy clients who can provide sponsorship for events, or other support. Journalists or actors between jobs may be willing to use their talents for the benefit of your charity.

KEY POINTS

- Generate as much free publicity as possible for your charity.
- Use all the methods available to you: all media, personal contacts of your own and of committee members and supporters.
- Designing and printing your own materials in-house can be cost-effective for small-scale operations.
- Try to generate sponsorship for publications such as newsletters or leaflets, or even your annual report.

CHAPTER SEVENTEEN

Monitoring and future plans

Your fundraising is running smoothly, income is exceeding expenditure, and your funding looks secure. Time to sit back and relax?

No! You can never afford to be complacent. As a local charity, you'll soon be aware if one of your major funders deserts the charity, and you may be able to take emergency action – perhaps using one of the techniques described in this book.

Sometimes, even when everything appears to be running smoothly, outgoings may start to exceed income without this being immediately noticeable. You must be constantly vigilant, and administration systems should be established and continuously monitored to keep control of income and expenditure.

The long-term success of your fundraising also depends upon the effectiveness of your public relations and advertising activities. Here again you must be sure that your reputation is sound and that the right message is getting across.

Financial monitoring

You may well be running several campaigns simultaneously: some continuous and some 'one-offs'. Not only should you know if you are making money overall, you must also be aware if any one of your campaigns is not meeting its target.

The following is duplicated from Chapter 3, The fundraising plan, because what was written at the beginning of this book is just as important at the end.

Projections

Your plan should end with your monthly financial projections, which you should work out with the help of your treasurer, broken down into:

- known income from covenants and other regular or predictable payments;
- projected income;
- the 'target' to achieve your budget (NB 'target' is always higher than 'budget');
- 'budget' is the amount you actually require;
- 'cash flow' – in practice the money will not come in at an even rate so the 'cash flow' projections will show how you are really doing against your target.

That was the plan: it is now important to check your monthly projections for real. You should carry out this exercise for every campaign and if you find that one is under-performing you should either take remedial action or decide not to carry on using that particular unprofitable technique.

Keep a careful watch on all expenses claims, broken down as far as possible against each campaign you are running. Some committee members may tend to submit over-zealous claims which can make all the difference between profit and loss.

Communications audit

Advertising

As mentioned in Chapter 16, Publicity techniques, you will not necessarily be spending a great deal of your budget on paid-for advertising. However, when you do, you can keep costs down by producing your own artwork on your computer. You are the custodian of your 'brand' so be sure that you are totally consistent and that every time your charity's name is displayed it is in the same distinctive style – your logo.

This is particularly important when you are doing joint promotions, and a local shop, or sometimes even a national advertiser, is doing co-operative advertising. Guard your corporate style ferociously.

Also be sure that your message is communicating. Check responses to your messages and if anyone is not getting the right story, don't blame them, but check that what you are saying is absolutely clear and that there is no possible ambiguity.

Public relations

Keep in constant contact with the editors of your local newspapers and with the news desks of the local radio stations. A key measurement of your success will be the amount of free and accurate publicity that you have generated and the strength of your reputation in your community.

Another measurement you might apply is to list all the people whom you regard as valuable contacts and ask yourself how many of them would greet you by your first name if you met them in the street!

You can use a questionnaire (such as the one suggested in Chapter 2) to check on your local fame. Suitably adapted, it could be used regularly, say once a year, to check on the status of your charity's profile. The importance of this cannot be overstressed because if no one has heard of your charity, it will be very hard to fundraise for it.

Correspondence

You should monitor all your charity's correspondence as this is another important gauge of how well you are communicating. You could use these criteria:

- number of letters received from the public;
- breakdown according to whether they are favourable, unfavourable or neither;
- the number containing constructive suggestions or practical offers of help.

Guard book

This is another important measure of the success of your communications because you should start a new guard book, or cuttings book, every year and you can compare one with another. Ideally the guard book should be a large blank book or giant photograph album, about 24 by 18 inches. Paste in it copies of every advertisement made for your charity, recording where and when it appeared. You should also keep press cuttings of every editorial mention of your charity in the press (and magazines) and make sure that every one is also clearly marked with where and when it appeared. A press cutting without attribution is hardly worth the paper it is printed on.

The guard book should also contain copies of all your leaflets, and posters (if necessary folded up or reduced in size). It is more difficult to keep a record of radio mentions, but if you keep in touch with the newsdesk you may be told when your story is going to be featured and they may even send you a cassette, or you can make your own recording.

Future plans

Finances

- Arrange to spend at least half a day each week with your treasurer.
- Are the funds under strict control, or can the ratio of spending to income be reduced?
- Is money being wasted on unnecessary expenditure?
- Are there any capital items which are not used which can be sold?

Fundraising techniques

Having established which have been the most successful fundraising activities, consider:

- whether they have 'worn out' or whether they will stand repetition;
- ideas for developing and improving the successful activities;
- any untried opportunities which might unlock previously untapped funds;
- organising a brainstorming session of the fundraising committee, with no fixed agenda, where ideas can be tossed around as some good concepts for the future might emerge.

Communications

- You have taken care to ensure that your advertising message is consistent and your logo is always used in its correct style. If it is obviously not doing its job then you should reconsider the charity's corporate style.
- You should be putting yourself around as much as possible. If you are not already a member you should join the local Chamber of Commerce and one or two other local organisations such as the Rotarians or the Round Table.
- Give talks and presentations to as many other local organisations as possible.

KEY POINTS

- Monitoring and evaluation of all your charity's attitudes should be a continuous process – you can never stop.
- Careful financial monitoring of each project is essential to ensure that expenditure is never out of control.
- Keep records of all advertisements and other communications concerning your charity.
- Always keep future plans updated and keep networking, maintaining and building personal contacts.

Bibliography

Reference books

British Rate and Data (BRAD). London: EMAP, 1977. (A monthly guide to media facts and figures – including lists of local media.)

Charities Digest. Family Welfare Association. London: Waterlow Information Services, 1997. (Alphabetical list of 2,500 medium and large charities and trusts.)

Debrett's People of Today. London: Debrett Peerage Sterling Publications, 1997.

Dimensions of the Voluntary Sector. West Malling, Kent: Charities Aid Foundation, 1997. (Formerly *Charity Trends* – future trends in charity giving.)

Directory of Grant-Making Trusts, 15th edition. West Malling, Kent: Charities Aid Foundation, 1997.

Facts and Figures on the Voluntary Sector. London: NCVO, 1994.

Guide to Company Giving. Paul Brown and John Smyth. London: Directory of Social Change, 1997.

Guide to the Major Trusts. Paul Brown and John Smyth. London: Directory of Social Change, 1997.

A Guide to Local Charitable Trusts. Volume I In the North of England; Volume II In the Midlands; Volume III In the South of England, David Casson. Volume IV In London, Karina Holly. London: Directory of Social Change, 1996.

Guidelines on Employing a Consultant. Stephen Lee. London: ICFM, 1995.

Jordans' Privately Owned Top 2000 Companies and *Jordans' Privately Owned Second Top 2000 Companies*. Bristol: Jordans, 1996. (Guide to top private companies – useful for local fundraising.)

The Major Companies Guide. Paul Brown, David Casson and John Smyth. London: Directory of Social Change, 1995.

Radio Authority Pocket Book. London: The Radio Authority. (Annual publication giving basic details on all Inner London Radio stations.)

The Sunday Times Book of the Rich. Philip Beresford (ed). London: Penguin, 1991.

Times 1000 Top Companies. M Allen (ed). London: The Times Books, 1997.

Whitaker's Almanac. London: Whitaker's. (The reference book on facts and figures, economic information, international and parliamentary facts.)

Who's Who. London: A & C Black, 1997. (People who matter in alphabetical order with address and telephone contact.)

Who Owns Whom. High Wycombe: Dun & Bradstreet, 1997. (Which companies own which companies.)

Willings Press Guide. Ann Hayes (ed). London: Reed Information Services, 1997. (Annual publication giving information on newspapers and periodicals.)

Contracts

Adirondack, Sandy and Macfarlane, Richard, *Getting Ready for Contracts*. London: Directory of Social Change, 1993.

Johnson, Richard, *Finance for Contracts*. London: Directory of Social Change and NCVO, 1994.

Finance and taxation

Caulfeild Grant, Ian, *The Treasurer's Handbook (a How To guide)*. West Malling, Kent: Charities Aid Foundation, 1996.

Guide to Charitable Giving and Taxation. Harpenden: Craigmyle, 1997.

Inland Revenue Publications: *Tax Relief for Charities* (IR 75), *Charities Series 1 Deed of Covenants, Gift Aid* (IR 113), *Sponsorship Payment* (IR 64), *Full Tax Details* (IR 75/65).

Fundraising for Charity. London: Tolley Publishing, 1996.

Fundraising

Allford, Marion, *Charity Appeals*. London: Dent/Directory of Social Change, 1993. (The author is well known for work on the Great Ormond Street Hospital Wishing Well appeal.)

Blume, Hilary, *Charity Shops*. London: Charities Advisory Trust, 1995.

Clarke, Sam and Norton, Michael, *The Complete Fundraising Handbook*. London: Directory of Social Change, 1997. (A key reference book on fundraising.)

Eastwood, Michael and Norton, Michael, *Writing Better Fundraising Applications*. London: Directory of Social Change, 1997.

Elischer, Tony, *Teach Yourself Fundraising*. London: Hodder & Stoughton, 1995.

Passingham, Sarah, *Tried and Tested Ideas for Raising Money Locally*. London: Directory of Social Change, 1994.

Passingham, Sarah, *Good Ideas for Raising Serious Money through Organising Events*. London: Directory of Social Change, 1995.

Passingham, Sarah, *Organising Local Events*. London: Directory of Social Change, 1995.

Prabhudas, Yasmin, *Image Building – Money Raising for Hard to Sell Groups*. London: Directory of Social Change, 1994.

Industry publications

See Appendix I for addresses and other contact details.

Charity Commission: many publications including *Charities and Fundraising*.

Institute of Charity Fundraising Managers (ICFM) publishes on: fundraising in schools, standard form of agreement between charities and fundraising consultants, reciprocal charity mailings, house-to-house collections (including lists of suppliers of collecting materials), telephone recruitment of collectors, the management of static, outward-bound telephone support.

Available to members of ICFM only: *Who's Who in Fundraising Directory* (gives lists of members and details of products and services to help fundraisers – published annually).

National Council for Voluntary Organisations (NCVO) publishes:

The Charities Acts 1992 and 1993: A Guide for Charities and Other Voluntary Organisations. London: NCVO, 1995.

Finding Funds: General Information on Funding for Voluntary Groups. London: NCVO, 1993.

Income Protection: A Guide for Voluntary Organisations. A Silley and Advice Development Team. London: NCVO, 1995.

VAT Guide for Voluntary Organisations. R Moore and A Silley. London: NCVO, 1995.

Law

Capper, Sally, *Is It Legal?* London: NCVO, 1988. (Guidance on legal issues for charities, such as licensing, and using children. Out of print, but a useful guide.)

Lloyd, Stephen and Middleton, Fiona, *The Charities Act Handbook*. London: Directory of Social Change, 1996.

Public relations, marketing and sponsorship

Ali, Moi, *The DIY Guide to PR*. London: Directory of Social Change, 1995.

Ali, Moi, *The DIY Guide to Marketing*. London: Directory of Social Change, 1996.

Hughes, Sarah (ed), *UK Press and Public Relations Annual*. London: Hollis Directories Ltd, 1997.

Sargenson, Rosemary, *Hollis Sponsorship and Donations Yearbook*. London: Hollis Directories Ltd, 1997.

Wells, Chris, *The DIY Guide to Charity Newsletters*. London: Directory of Social Change, 1996. (For charities, voluntary organisations and community groups.)

Volunteers

Forbes, Duncan, Hayes, Ruth and Reason, Jackie, *Voluntary but not Amateur*. London: London Voluntary Service Council, 1994.

NVCO, *Who can Help Voluntary Organisations*. London: NCVO Information Sheet. (This previously annual publication is currently out of print, but an out-of-date edition may still be useful.)

Appendix I Sources of information and training

This appendix lists useful addresses, periodicals and sources of training.

Useful addresses

Action and Employment in the Community
8 Stratton Street
London W1X 5PD
Tel (0171) 629 2209

Age Concern England
A major national charity for older people.
Astral House
1268 London Road
London SW16 4ER
Tel (0181) 679 8000

Alexandra Rose Day (ARD)
ARD arranges collections for the smaller charities.
1 Castelnau
London SW13 9RP
Tel (0181) 748 4824

Association of Arts Fundraisers
38 Convent Road
Broadstairs
Kent CT10 3BE
Tel (01843) 862743

Association for Business Sponsorship of the Arts (ABSA)
60 Gainsford Street
London SE1 2NY
Tel (0171) 378 8143

Association of Fundraising Consultants (AFC)
Top fundraising companies and consultants.

The Grove
Harpenden
Herts AL5 1AH
Tel (01582) 762446

British Association of Settlements and Social Action Centres
An umbrella group for settlements.

First Floor
Winchester House
11 Cranmer Road
London SW9 6EJ
Tel (0171) 735 1075

British Telecom

Secondment Manager
Room A302
Newgate Street
London EC1A 7AJ
Tel (0171) 356 5369

Business in the Community
Organisation for business people or companies supporting charities in a variety of ways.

44 Baker Street
London W1M 1DH
Tel (0171) 224 1600

Business Research Group

BRG Direct
55 Morrab Road
Penzance
Cornwall PR18 4EX
Tel (01736) 351681

Chapter One Group Ltd
Offers direct mail services, among others.

Green Lane
Tewkesbury
Glos GL20 8EZ
Tel (01684) 850040

Charities Advisory Trust

Radius Works
Back Lane
London NW3 1HL
Tel (0171) 794 9835

Charities Aid Foundation
*Major charitable group – promotes
various tax-effective methods of
giving, offers annual conference
advice and publishes books and
magazines for the charity sector.*

Kings Hill
West Malling
Kent ME19 4TA
Tel (01732) 520000

Charity Commission
*Official regulatory body
for charities.*

St Albans House
57–60 Haymarket
London SW1 4QX
Tel (0171) 210 3000

Charity Projects/Comic Relief
Organisers of Red Nose Day.

74 New Oxford Street
London WC1A 1EU
Tel (0171) 436 1122

**Community Development
Foundation**
Supports community initiatives.

60 Highbury Grove
London N5 2AG
Tel (0171) 226 5375

Community Radio Association

15 Paternoster Row
Sheffield S1 2BX
Tel (0114) 279 5219

Cornhill Insurance plc
*Offers insurance services
to the voluntary sector.*

32 Cornhill
London EC3V 3LJ
Tel (0171) 626 5410

Data Protection Register
Oversees the Data Protection Act.

Springfield House
Water Lane
Wilmslow
Cheshire SK9 5AF
Tel (01625) 535777

Direct Marketing Association
*Trade association for the direct
marketing and mail industry.*

1 Oxendon Street
London SW1Y 4EE
Tel (0171) 321 2525

Directory of Social Change (DSC)
Providers of a conference and training, publishers for the charity and voluntary sector.

24 Stephenson Way
London NW1 2DP
Tel (0171) 209 5151

Dorincourt Industries
Printing services: a unit of Queen Elizabeth's Foundation for disabled people.

Bradmere House
Kingston Road
Leatherhead
Surrey KT22 7NA
Tel (01372) 361381

Dun & Bradstreet Ltd
Suppliers of business information.

Holmers Way Farm
High Wycombe
Bucks HP12 4UL
Tel (01494) 422299

Ecclesiastical Insurance Group
A charity offering insurance services to charities and voluntary organisations.

Beaufort House
Brunswick Road
Gloucester GL1 1JZ
Tel (01452) 528533

The Factary
Researchers into sources of funds – especially trusts – local knowledge a speciality.

The Coach House
2 Upper York Street
Bristol BS2 8QN
Tel (0117) 924 0663

Federation of Independent Advice-giving Centres

13 Stockwell Road
London SW9 9AU
Tel (0171) 274 1839

Funderfinder
Funderfinder *is a software package for organisations seeking support from trusts.*

65 Raglan Road
Leeds LS2 9DZ
Tel (01132) 433008

Grand Metropolitan Trust
Supports charities, a member of Business in the Community, offers volunteer service.

20 St James' Square
London SW1Y 4JC
Tel (0171) 321 6000

The Grand Order (Masons)

The Provincial Grand
   Secretary
Warwickshire Masonic
   Temple
Station Road
Edgbaston
Birmingham B16 9SB
Tel (0121) 454 4422

Health & Safety Executive

Rose Court
2 Southwark Bridge
London SE1 9HS
Tel (0171) 717 6000

Help the Aged
Advises on funding for
'grey' charities.

St James' Walk
London EC1R 0BE
Tel (0171) 253 0253

HM Customs & Excise

4th Floor West
New King's Beam House
22 Upper Ground
London SE1 9PJ
Tel (0171) 620 1313

Hollis Directories Ltd
Publishers of yearbooks
and annuals.

Harlequin House
7 High Street
Teddington
Middx TW11 8EL
Tel (0181) 977 7711

**Inland Revenue
(England, Wales and
Northern Ireland)**

Ground Floor
South-west Wing
Bush House
Strand
London WC2B 4RD
Tel (0171) 438 6420/
         6425

Inland Revenue (Scotland)

Trinity Park House
South Trinity Road
Edinburgh EH5 3SD
Tel (0131) 552 6255

**Institute of Charity
Fundraising Managers
(ICFM)**
*Professional body for the
fundraising industry – one special
interest group is Fundraisers in
Small Organisations.*

Market Towers
1 Nine Elms Lane
London SW8 5NQ
Tel (0171) 627 3436

Institute of Public Relations
*Professional body for the public
relations industry.*

The Old Trading House
15 Northburgh Street
London EC1V 0PR
Tel (0171) 253 5151

Leading Edge
*Promotional computer products
for fundraising.*

Bank House
65 Fore Street
Buckfastleigh
Devon TQ11 0BS
Tel (01364) 644244

Lions Club International

267 Alcester Road South
Kings Heath
Birmingham B14 6BT
Tel (0121) 441 4544

**Local Government
Information Unit**
*Provides comprehensive advice
on up-to-date issues relating to
local government.*

1–5 Bath Street
London EC1V 9QQ
Tel (0171) 608 1051

Market Research Society

15 Northburgh Street
London EC1V 0AH
Tel (0171) 490 4911

Media Trust
*Assists charities to work with
the media.*

56 Whitfield Street
London W1P 5RN
Tel (0171) 637 4747

National Association of Councils of Voluntary Service (NACVS)
Umbrella group for Councils of Voluntary Service.

3rd Floor
Arundel Court
177 Arundel Street
Sheffield S1 2NU
Tel (0114) 278 6636

National Association of Round Tables

The Secretary
Marchesi House
Embassy Drive
Birmingham B15 1TP
Tel (0121) 456 4402

National Council for Voluntary Organisations

Regent's Wharf
8 All Saints Street
London N1 9RL
Tel (0171) 713 6161

National Federation of Women's Institutes

104 New Kings Road
London SW6 4LY
Tel (0171) 371 9300

National Payroll Giving Services (NPGS)

1 Bridge Chambers
Barnstaple
North Devon EX31 1HB
Tel (01271) 328609

Newspaper Society
Promotes the regional press.

Bloomsbury House
74–77 Great Russell Street
London WC1B 3DA
Tel (0171) 636 7014

Peeks of Bournemouth
Provides games and sideshow equipment for hire.

Riverside Lane
Tuckton
Bournemouth
Dorset BH6 3LD
Tel (01202) 417777

Personal Telephone Fundraising
Telephone fundraising experts (suppliers of the script in Chapter 6).

97 Church Street
Brighton
Sussex BN1 1EX
Tel (01273) 698697

The Radio Authority

Holbrook House
14 Great Queen Street
Holborn
London WC2B 5DG
Tel (0171) 430 2724

Retired Executives Action
Clearing House (REACH)
Source of good-quality
professional volunteers.

Bear Wharf
27 Bankside
London SE1 9ET
Tel (0171) 928 0452

Rotary International
Britain and Ireland

The Secretary
Kingswater Road
Alcester
Warks B49 6BP
Tel (01789) 765411

Royal Association for
Disability and Rehabilitation
(RADAR)
Umbrella group for charities
for people with disabilities.

250 City Road
London EC1V 2AS
Tel (0171) 250 3222

Smee & Ford Ltd
Experts in the legacy field. Provide
a will-reporting service.

2nd Floor
St George's House
195–203 Waterloo Road
London SE1 8UX
Tel (0171) 928 4050

Soroptimist International

The Secretary
127 Wellington Road South
Stockport
Cheshire SK1 3TS
Tel (0161) 480 7686

Sports Council
Government liaison body
for the sports world.

16 Upper Woburn Place
London WC1H 0QP
Tel (0171) 388 1277

Syndicate Services:
Community Service Volunteers
237 Pentonville Road
London N1 9NJ
Tel (0171) 278 6601

Townswomen's Guild
Chamber of Commerce
    House
7 Harborne Road
Edgbaston
Birmingham B15 3DA
Tel (0121) 456 3435

Voluntary Organisations
Internet Service
1 Eton Garages
Belsize Park
London NW1 5NR
Tel (0171) 435 5787

Volunteer Centre UK
Source of volunteers and advice.
Carriage Row
183 Eversholt Street
London NW1 1BO
Tel (0171) 388 9888

Webb Ivory
Gifts and articles for sale through
charities.
Preston
Lancs PRO 2QX
Tel (01254) 302266

Periodicals

The following publications provide insight into fundraising and the developments within the ever-changing charity world.

Charity
The trade magazine for charities,
which discusses most topical issues.
Centurion Press Ltd
Centurion House
High Street
Rickmansworth
Herts WD3 1ER
Tel (01923) 891044

Charity Times
Business and financial management journal for charities. Builds a picture of the economy.

Perspective Publishing Ltd
408 The Fruit & Wool
  Exchange
Brushfield Street
London E1 6EP
Tel (0171) 426 0101

Charity World
Financial and legal matters of current concern to charity decision-makers at all levels.

Space Works
70 Queen's Head Street
Islington
London N1 8NG
Tel (0171) 369 1934

Corporate Citizen
Details of company, statutory and EC support.

Directory of Social Change
24 Stephenson Way
London NW1 2DP
Tel (0171) 209 5151

Professional Fundraiser
The professional journal for fundraisers, which can provide the non-professional with trade ideas.

DRM Ltd
Post Office Walk
Fore Street
Hertford
Herts SE14 1DR
Tel (01992) 501177

Sponsorship Newsletter
Bi-monthly update on sponsorship.

Hollis Directories Ltd
Harlequin House
7 High Street
Teddington
Middx TW11 8EL
Tel (0181) 977 7711

Third Sector
Trade magazine – slanted towards the smaller charity.

Arts Publishing
  International Ltd
4 Assam Street
London E1 7QS
Tel (0171) 247 0066

Trust Monitor
*Developments in the trust world,
including new trusts, changes in
trust guidelines, trustees,
correspondence. Bi-monthly.*

Directory of Social Change
24 Stephenson Way
London NW1 2DP
Tel (0171) 209 5151

The Voice
*Not a charity publication but
can be an excellent way to obtain
volunteers. Read by many ethnic
minorities.*

Voice Group Ltd
370 Coldharbour Lane
London SW9 8PL
Tel (0171) 737 7377

**Will to Charity: Charities
by Counties**
*Lists charities, and is circulated
free to funeral directors and
solicitors.*

Will to Charity Ltd
Pandemonium House
Halebourne Lane
Chobham
Surrey GU24 8SL
Tel (01276) 856622

Sources of training

Charities Aid Foundation
Organises conferences.

Kings Hill
West Malling
Kent ME19 4TA
Tel (01732) 520000

Directory of Social Change
*Courses on all aspects of fundraising
and charity management.*

24 Stephenson Way
London NW1 2DP
Tel (0171) 209 4130

Fresh Fields Training
*Training on using the telephone
for obtaining donations is among
the skills offered.*

The Little House
Bath Road
Norton St Philip
Bath BA3 6LP
Tel (01373) 834497

Institute of Charity Fundraising Managers (ICFM)
The professional body for fundraising, offering professional qualifications and training from assistant to director levels.

Market Towers
1 Nine Elms Lane
London SW8 5NQ
Tel (0171) 627 3436

Kelly Consultancy
Fundraising training.

42 Middleton Drive
Pinner
Middx HA5 2PG
Tel (0181) 868 0207

Media Trust
Offers media training by professionals to match your needs.

56 Whitfield Street
London W1P 5RN
Tel (0171) 637 4747

The Midas Partnership
Training covers trusts and European funding.

Thatch Cottage
23 Church Road
Great Stukeley
Huntingdon
Cambs PE17 5AL
Tel (01480) 431112

National Council for Voluntary Organisations (NCVO)
Advice and training for the voluntary sector, especially for the smaller charities.

Regent's Wharf
8 All Saints Street
London N1 9RL
Tel (0171) 713 6161

The Projects Company
In-house training on fundraising and management techniques.

William Lodge
Church Road
High Beach
Loughton
Essex IG10 4AJ
Tel (0181) 502 2327

Prospecting for Gold
*Training in fundraising, both
in- and out-house. Also known
as Charity Consultants Ltd.*

Little Holme
Station Road
Shiplake
Henley-on-Thames
Oxon RG9 3JS
Tel (0118) 940 1016

Smee & Ford Ltd
*Training in all aspects of legacy
fundraising.*

2nd Floor
St George's House
195–203 Waterloo Road
London SE1 8UX
Tel (0171) 928 4050

Jennie Whiting
*Training in fundraising techniques,
especially organising collections.
Probably the expert in the field.*

Mistletoe Cottage
29 New Cut
Layer-de-la-Haye
Colchester
Essex CO2 0EG
Tel (01206) 734572

Appendix II Legislation

This appendix includes key elements of local authority licensing requirements, the Data Protection Act 1984, and the Charities Act 1961 (amended 1993).

Other acts of Parliament referred to in this book are the Commercial Radio Act 1990, and the NHS and Community Care Act 1990. The full texts are available from The Stationery Office.

Advertising is governed by the ASA and must comply with the ASA Code of Practice.

Advertising Standards Authority (ASA)
Brook House
Torrington Place
London WC1E 7HW
Tel (0171) 580 5555

Local authority licensing

Entertainment

Councils must consider every application made for an annual entertainment licence. The applicant for a new entertainment licence has to advertise by:

- a notice exhibited at the premises concerned for not less than 28 days;
- a notice published in a local newspaper on sale at local newsagents.

Advertisement by these means is also required of applications for amendment of existing annual licences if the grant of the application might lead to noise and disturbance. An applicant does not have to advertise for the renewal of a licence.

Collections

Collections in public places must be licensed by the Metropolitan Police if in Greater London and by local councils elsewhere.

Exhibitions

You will need a licence for sporting displays such as archery or judo.

Licensing officer

Local authorities have licensing departments, and the licensing officer can be a useful source of information. Guidance notes are produced and can be sent to you free of charge. Local authorities are essentially concerned with public performances, collections, and lotteries or raffles.

Food

Health regulations and food-handling are dealt with by the council environmental health department. Regulations in this area are always strictly enforced by environmental health officers, and it is worth discussing with the department any function dealing with food. Notes for guidance are produced.

Liquor

An occasional liquor licence is required for unlicensed premises (such as a church) serving liquor to the public. The magistrates office should be applied to.

Children

It is technically against the law for children younger than 16 years of age to be involved directly in fundraising.

Shops

It is recommended that charity shops display a notice saying that all profits are covenanted to the charity concerned. All goods must be donated. Charity law states that charities cannot engage in trading directly, and therefore most charities set up a trading company covenanting all profits to charity.

Telephone appeals

The following information should be clearly communicated during the telephone appeal: the name of the person making the call, registration and name of the charity, the purpose of the call. People making donations of more than £50 should be allowed a 'cooling off' period, and no calls can be made after 9pm.

By law you must monitor appeal calls and will need to complete a control form. Your local BT office can give advice on this. The form must state the volunteer's name, the contact, their telephone number, the time of the call, any donation made, the method of payment, and any call back.

The Data Protection Act 1984

The Act requires all those who store personal details on a computer to register their use of that data with the Data Protection Registrar. The purpose of the Act is to protect the rights of the individual about whom data is obtained, stored or supplied, rather than the rights of the data user.

Scope of the Act

The Act applies only to automatically processed information – broadly speaking, information that is processed by a computer. It does not cover information that is held and processed manually, for example in ordinary paper files.

The Act does not cover all computerised information but only that which relates to living individuals. So, for example, it does not cover information that relates only to a company or organisation and not to an individual.

'Personal data' are items of information recorded on a computer about living, identifiable individuals. Statements of fact and expressions of opinion about an individual are personal data, but an indication of the data user's intention towards the individual is not.

A 'data subject' is an individual to whom personal data relate. 'Data users' are people or organisations who control the contents and use of a collection of personal data. A data user will usually be a company, corporation or other organisation, but it is possible for an individual to be a data user.

Computer bureaux are people or organisations who process personal data for users or who allow data users to process personal data on their computers.

Data protection principles

Registered data users must comply with the data protection principles in relation to the personal data they hold. The principles broadly state that personal data shall:

- be obtained and processed fairly and lawfully;
- be held for those purposes and be disclosed only to those people described in the register entry;
- be adequate, relevant and not excessive in relation to the purpose for which they are held;
- be accurate and, where necessary, kept up to date;
- be held no longer than is necessary for the registered purpose;
- be surrounded by proper security.

The Registrar can serve three types of notice:

- An enforcement notice requiring the data user to take specified action to comply with the particular principles. Failure to comply with the notice is a criminal offence.
- A de-registration notice, cancelling the whole or part of a data user's register entry. The data user would then be committing an offence if they continued to treat personal data subject to the notice as though they were registered.

- A transfer prohibition notice, preventing the data user from transferring personal data overseas if the Registrar is satisfied that the transfer is likely to lead to a principle being broken. Failure to comply with such a notice is a criminal offence.

A person on whom a notice is served is entitled to appeal against the Registrar's decision to the Data Protection Tribunal.

Charities Act 1961 (amended 1993)

The Charities Act is a complex piece of legislation. Part II deals specifically with fundraising. The ICFM produces guidelines on the Act and the Charity Commission Fundraising Department will always answer questions. Of concern to the local fundraiser are the following aspects of the Act:

- All printed material, including T-shirts, must have the charity's logo, registration number and name.
- Collectors must have identification and the charity's agreement to their collecting.
- The local authority must give permission for collections to take place.
- An annual report and accounts must be produced and sent to the Charity Commissioners.

The Act defines a commercial participator as one who:

- carries on for gain a business other than a fundraising business;
- in the course of that business, engages in any promotional venture in the course of which it is represented that charitable contributions are to be given to or applied for the benefit of the institution.

A fundraiser is defined as: Any person (apart from a charitable institution) who carries on a fundraising business or any person who for reward solicits money or other property for the benefit of a charitable institution, if they do so otherwise than in the course of any fundraising venture undertaken by a person falling within a fundraising business.

Appendix III Sample letters

Letter to a friend from fundraising chairperson

Dear Bill

I am writing to you as a fellow Thespian.

Did you know that in Porchester there are some 3,000 young people without homes – sleeping in doorways, on friends' floors and in outbuildings. And as many again sleep in the surrounding countryside, but the problem is not so apparent there as it is in London. Recently, after returning from my US tour, I became involved in the Porchester Homeless Project.

In fact I was so impressed by their work that I agreed to become their Patron.

As you know, if you have the right skills there are plenty of technology jobs in the Thames Valley. We plan to build a hostel in 1998 for our young people, and to give counselling sessions. Many of the young people come from families which are dysfunctional in some way, and, sadly, most have little faith in the world, especially in people.

Remembering the marvellous work you did for Reading's Guys and Dolls Home, I am asking for a nice fat donation. Do you remember the celebrity golf day we endured together?

In order to get the project off the ground I need to raise £70,000 by Easter. I have donated £9,000. Jo and Anna have pledged

£2,000 and other pledges amount to £20,000, notably from Sir George.

We plan a celebrity night at the Podium Theatre for supporters. The old crowd will be there, plus the cameras.

Attached is the annual report and accounts (I know what a stickler you are on figures), details of the charity and the project.

Looking forward to your support.

With best wishes

Letter to a trust

Dear Mr Smith

GRANT APPLICATION

We are a local charity, Charlie's Project – a refuge for abused women and their children. We are seeking your support for an innovative project providing emotional support and training to help our clients gain skills to generate employment.

The Need
Forty per cent of those who come to us are receiving housing benefit, most are unemployed, many are from ethnic minorities. The need is to extend our premises so that more facilities can be provided. A detailed plan of the proposed project is enclosed. We wish to improve the lives of some 39 women each year.

Funding Support
We expect to start building in March 1998. Our clients will be involved with making curtains, decorating the premises and, in one case, making the furniture. We believe that this project is a model way in which local women can work together, relate to each other and the neighbourhood, and start to be members of the community. Because of this, Barnbridge Local Authority has agreed a grant of £20,000 for three years. Laing Housing has contributed £10,000 and Tudor Trust £10,000. Other pledges amount to £27,000. Due to gifts in kind and offers of free labour we should be able to build the hostel for only £120,000.

We would like you to ask your Trustees to award us a grant – not only for the funding but because your support would be such an encouragement to other funders.

Please do not hesitate to visit the project. I should be delighted to show you round our existing building and to offer you lunch in our Riverside Cafe – run by clients.

Yours sincerely

Letter to companies from another company chairperson

Dear Friend

The Children of Grey Camp Need Your Help

As a growing Bath business, we thought long and hard about how to manage our charitable giving. We decided that rather than hand out small amounts to many charities, we would develop a close relationship with one organisation where we could make a real difference and with whom we could develop a fellow feeling.

I spent some time visiting organisations that were helping locally, to find out which could use our assistance. One of the places I visited was Grey Camp and I knew immediately that this was the local group that deserved every penny that we could give.

Since then we have actively supported Grey Camp and we have been able to help them to develop relationships with many other organisations who have been generous enough to support their amazingly worthwhile work.

A Unique and Caring Organisation
Grey Camp is run by George Grey in order to provide training for local young people who are habitual offenders. The results are impressive – from young tearaways with no future George can cite those who have become lecturers, businessmen, and even a film producer.

*In 20 years 2,000 youngsters have passed through George's
care. He started as teacher in the East End of London and came
to Bath as a clergyman.*

Why I Am Writing to You Now
*This letter is to ask URGENTLY for your support: £20,000
is needed to make vital repairs. If these are not done within
12 months the Camp must close – and some 200 local
youngsters will be out of control.*

*I am afraid that I have attached with this letter a considerable
amount of reading material as follows:*

– *Background to Grey Camp;*
– *Details of the fundraising project;*
– *Police and Social Services Report.*

*If you can make time to read this, I promise you will not regret it.
Enclosed is a donation slip together with details of tax-effective
ways of giving. George or one of the fundraising team would be
delighted to show you around Grey Camp. We all know you will
be impressed.*

Yours

Draft legacy response letter

Dear Mrs Jones

*Thank you very much indeed for contacting us about your
wish to support our charitable work with a gift in your will.*

*I am delighted by your generosity although I naturally hope
that any provision you make for us will be long in the future.
You have been a valued donor for a number of years now and
it is heartening to know that you are keen to help us in the
longer term with a legacy.*

*The most beneficial way of doing this is to leave your chosen gift
to us in an unrestricted way so that when the time comes we can
apply the monies to the areas of greatest need.*

Although you can write your own will at home or use a form from any leading stationers it is preferable to consult a solicitor, who will be able to answer any legal or technical questions you may have.

It is equally important to phrase your legacy in the right way, and the following wording is offered for your guidance:

"I give devise and bequeath to the TIDAL Hospice of Dover Road, Anytown, Midshire (Registered Charity No. 123456) the sum of £..... (pounds) or the whole (or a share) of my residuary estate for its general charitable purposes and I declare that the receipt of the Treasurer or other proper officer of the Hospice shall be a sufficient discharge therefore."

In practical terms it may be better to divide your whole estate, in whatever proportions you choose, between all your beneficiaries since cash sums will progressively lose their value unless you regularly update your will.

If you wish to make any specific provision in connection with your intended legacy to us I shall be more than happy to discuss the appropriate wording with you. I am here to help in any way I can.

With my renewed thanks and very best wishes.

Yours sincerely

Letter to local donors

Major advances in the fight against cancer

Your £10 could help us to help local young children stay alive.

Dear Mrs Benham

You must have heard of St Cross Hospital for young children with CANCER. If you thought they came to us to die, please think again. Tremendous advances have been made in the treatment of cancer, bringing new hope to many children and their parents.

The results from our medical team are so encouraging. Over the last twenty years, the number of child cancer cases has been halved. Now St Cross Hospital's team can offer children the hope of life, BUT only with your help can we bring more local children into our care. The non-specialist hospitals in the area cannot cope with the need – not only of this town but of the county.

We know some children die through lack of care. Just £10 from you could make a difference; £100 could sponsor a child's bed for a month; and £1,000 could do so for a year. If we work together we can save or extend so many lives.

May I suggest you call in and see us at our Open Day on Saturday 12 June? We are looking forward to welcoming our friends from 10am, and this will also give you the opportunity to realise why we are making the Group 24,000 appeal – in fact we need the money not only to build our work saving young lives but just to carry on. If you cannot come on 12 June then please fill in the coupon for as much as you can afford – call in with the envelope or drop it in the post.

YOUR HELP IS DESPERATELY NEEDED.

Thank you for your support.

Matron/Administration

Appendix IV Taxation

This is a general guide to taxation (including VAT) issues for local charities; full details are available from the Inland Revenue and other sources listed in the bibliography to this volume.

Deeds of covenant

A deed of covenant is a legal document by which a promise is made to pay a fixed sum of money at a particular time of year, usually once a year. For tax purposes a covenant should last for a period of more than three years: this is why most charitable covenants are for four years.

Covenanted payments to charity are treated in a special way for tax purposes. Covenantors who are tax payers can get tax relief for the payments they make, so in effect they give more than the cost to themselves. The charity must reclaim the tax from the Inland Revenue.

Gift Aid

Gift Aid is a tax relief for single outright cash gifts. The gift must be at least £250 after basic tax is taken out. A payment is made to the charity (net of basic tax) and the charity is given a certificate so that it can claim tax back from the Inland Revenue.

Secondment of employees

Secondment is defined as 'the secondment of an employee to work for a charity on a temporary basis'. Any costs incurred in connection with this employment (including salary) are allowed as a deduction in calculating the seconding company's trading profits for tax purposes.

Payroll giving

Payroll giving is a way for employees to give to charity directly from their pay, to obtain tax relief on their payments. Up to £900 in any tax year can be given. Employers deduct the money from pay and hand it over to an agency charity, which will pass it on to the charity or charities chosen. The employer deducts the gift from pay before PAYE tax is calculated.

Events exempt from taxation

The events which are exempt are: banquets, gala nights, film premieres, theatre first nights, and concerts which take place during a single day. Charities can hold a number of events of similar nature in one year. Annual concerts may still qualify for exemption. Coffee mornings and similar events are exempt if they are low key: if an event is raising funds locally, the determining factor should be the likely impact of the fundraising events on normal commercial activity.

If you need further information or advice contact your local VAT office (details are listed in the telephone book under 'Customs and Excise'). The local knowledge of each office makes it best placed to answer your queries.

Sponsorship payments

Tax relief is available for payments made to sponsor a charitable activity, provided that payments are not of a capital nature and are made wholly and exclusively for the purpose of the payer's trade.

Trading profits

A charity's trading profits are exempt from taxation so long as:

- the trade carries out a primary purpose for the charity;
- the work is done mainly for the beneficiaries of the charity.

Fundraising activities may or may not be a trade:

- the realisation of donated goods is not a trade;
- in general, a non-charitable trade should not be carried out directly by the charity.

Shops are a particular case. You will need to discuss Council Tax with your local authority. See also the section of this appendix (below) on VAT.

Legacies

Any gift to a charity under a will is free of inheritance tax. (See Inland Revenue booklets IHT2 and IHT3 for further details.)

Value Added Tax (VAT)

VAT is a tax on goods and services which is collected by registered persons and paid to the government of the United Kingdom on a quarterly basis. Registration is required for organisations with business income exceeding an annual threshold set by the annual Finance Act (£48,000 in 1997/98). The registration will include all associated bodies together with the main charity, for example branches and local groups. A charity must decide whether its activities are 'business' or 'non-business':

- Donations, legacies or other voluntary contributions from the public are outside the scope of VAT.
- Grants which are not the consideration for services rendered can also be treated as non-business income and outside the scope of VAT.
- Services provided free of charge are exempt from VAT.

- The sale of donated goods is taxable unless when made by any charity or by any taxable person covenanting all the profits from the sale of donated goods to a charity.

- Brochures – no less than 50 per cent of the total number of advertisements in publications such as annual reports must clearly be from private individuals. If the brochure is supplied as a one-off fundraising event it may be exempt.

Sponsorship and VAT

If a charity receives a donation, for example from a company, and merely provides a simple acknowledgement of the sponsor's contribution, the donation is outside the scope of VAT. If, however, the company receives some benefit, for example free tickets to an event, then the contribution is regarded as the consideration for a supply made in the course of business to the charity, and therefore subject to VAT.

About CAF
·········

CAF, Charities Aid Foundation, is a registered charity with a unique mission – to increase the substance of charity in the UK and overseas. It provides services that are both charitable and financial which help donors make the most of their giving and charities make the most of their resources.

Many of CAF's publications reflect the organisation's purpose: *Dimensions of the Voluntary Sector* offers the definitive financial overview of the sector, while the *Directory of Grant Making Trusts* provides the most comprehensive source of funding information available.

As an integral part of its activities, CAF works to raise standards of management in voluntary organisations. This includes the making of grants by its own Grants Council, sponsorship of the Charity Annual Report and Accounts Awards, seminars, training courses and the Charities Annual Conference, the largest regular gathering of key people from within the voluntary sector. In addition, Charitynet is now established as the leading Internet site on voluntary action.

For decades, CAF has led the way in developing tax-effective services to donors, and these are now used by more than 150,000 individuals and 2,000 of the UK's leading companies. Many are also using CAF's CharityCard, the world's first debit card designed exclusively for charitable giving. CAF's unique range of investment and administration services for charities includes the CafCash High Interest Cheque Account, two common investment funds for longer-term investment and a full appeals and subscription management service.

CAF's activities are not limited to the UK, however. Increasingly, CAF is looking to apply the same principles and develop similar services internationally, in its drive to increase the substance of charity across the world.

CAF
Kings Hill
West Malling
Kent ME19 4TA

Telephone +44 (0) 1732 520000

Fax +44 (0) 1732 520001

Web site http://www.charitynet.org

E-mail cafpubs@caf.charitynet.org

Other publications from CAF
·········

A series of one-stop guides on a variety of core activities, the
titles appearing in the CAF 'How To' series are designed to
provide both volunteers supporting smaller charities – in either
an official or an unofficial capacity – and inexperienced salaried
staff with practical information and guidance on good practice.

The Treasurer's Handbook A guide for small voluntary
organisations *Ian Caulfeild Grant*
··················
ISBN 1–85934–018–0 £7.95
Published August 1996

Recent legislation has reinforced the crucial role of the treasurer
in voluntary organisations of all sizes, whilst the introduction of
the SORP is intended to lead to a greater uniformity of practice
throughout the sector.

As a treasurer's duties become more onerous, their
personal, legal liability for the 'prudent management' of their
organisation is thrown sharply into relief. Yet many volunteer
treasurers do not have even a basic understanding of book-
keeping activities.

In straightforward language, avoiding financial jargon, *The
Treasurer's Handbook* outlines a treasurer's key tasks, proposes
appropriate procedures and explains the basics of financial
management.

Applying to a Grant Making Trust A guide for fundraisers
Anne Villemur

ISBN 1–85934–033–4 £7.95
Published January 1997

Grant-making trusts of all sizes complain that many of
the funding applications which they receive fail either to
match their stated funding priorities or to provide a coherent
explanation of the project or programme for which support
is being sought. Consequently, they are ineligible for
consideration.

In response to this situation, and drawing on the author's years
of experience as editor of *The Directory of Grant Making Trusts*,
this book provides step-by-step guidance on drawing up a well-
rounded 'case for support' which contains all the information
which trustees require when considering an application.

Including practical advice on project-costing, selecting
appropriate trusts and chasing up applications, *Applying to a
Grant Making Trust* is the companion volume to the *DGMT*
which users have long been demanding.

The Directory of Grant Making Trusts 1997–98 15th edition

ISBN 1–85934–025–3 £69.95 (2 volumes)
Published February 1997

Acknowledged as the definitive guide to grant-making trusts
in the UK, this directory enables fundraisers to pinpoint those
trusts whose funding objectives match their own particular
project or area of work.

Split into two volumes for the first time, and containing the
details of over 500 additional trusts, the 1997–98 edition has
undergone a complete design overhaul in order to make the
information it contains even more straightforward and
accessible.

The indices which 'lead' the user to the most relevant trusts
have also been radically improved and an entirely new
classification of types of beneficiary has been adopted.

Particularly significantly, the listing of trusts by beneficial area has been reorganised in order to highlight regional funding preferences more clearly.

These improvements will enable fundraisers to obtain an even more detailed understanding of the future funding policies of the trusts listed and thereby to tailor their requests for support more accurately – so reducing the time and money wasted on inappropriate appeals.

Grant-making trusts made grants in excess of £700 million in 1995. The *DGMT* is designed to act as the lifeline between good causes in desperate need of support and this rich vein of funding.

Grantseeker The interactive CD-ROM for fundraisers
ISBN 1–85934–032 –6 £150 + £26.25 VAT
Published August 1997

Drawing on CAF's years of experience as publisher of *The Directory of Grant Making Trusts*, *Grantseeker* is the tailor-made solution to the information needs of trust fundraisers in the electronic age.

Fully interactive, the specially designed search engine will scan the entire DGMT database in a matter of seconds on the basis of a user's own selection criteria and generate a ranked 'hit list' of trusts whose funding preferences match their project or cause. Selection criteria particular to the CD are details of grant type.

Taking full advantage of the 'added value' available via an electronic search tool, Grantseeker offers a more sophisticated matching service than can be provided by traditional methods, enabling fundraisers to save weeks of effort and frustration. A simple hypertext link can provide them with a complete *DGMT* entry on a potential funder within moments of loading the CD. The days of ultimate dependence on a paper-based directory are over.

The sample grant data from selected trusts, published separately in the Grants Index, appear in the full trust entries featured in Grantseeker.

Designed for use by fundraisers with little or no experience of electronic directories, as well as the more technically minded, Grantseeker provides step-by-step instructions on every stage of the search process, backed by comprehensive help files. Even the most confirmed Luddite should not be intimidated!

Grantseeker runs under Windows 3.1 or Windows 95.

Trustees Index

ISBN 1–85934–039–3 £14.95
Published February 1997

The importance of establishing 'who knows who' at an early stage in a fundraising campaign is widely recognised. In certain circumstances, a quiet word in an appropriate ear can be worth dozens of well-researched applications for support. And privately most grant-seekers acknowledge that some of their biggest donations are received from trusts where a trustee is personally known to a member of their appeal committee.

The Trustees Index provides an alphabetical listing of all the trustees whose names are held on the main DGMT database along with details of the trusts with which they are associated. Designed to be highly accessible, this directory will make it easy for fundraisers to identify the details of particular individuals and to use the data revealed to develop their own 'hit list' of trusts to be approached.

Grants Index

ISBN 1–85934–026–1 £14.95
Published February 1997

Experienced grant-seekers know that while a large number of trusts may state that they are open to applications for support from organisations working in many different fields, there are many which, in reality, make donations only to particular causes.

Published as a companion volume to the *DGMT*, the *Grants Index* provides comprehensive information on actual grants leading trusts have made in the recent past. Based on information received from the trusts themselves, the sample data provided is intended to be representative of the range of all donations made.

Used in conjunction with the relevant entry in the *DGMT*, the *Grants Index* will enable fundraisers to build a more detailed profile of individual trusts and consequently target their applications more accurately.

Index